7/90

# CALLING, TRACY!

DATE DUE

**JAMES VAN HISE** writes about film, television and comic book history. He has written numerous books on these subjects, including BATMANIA, THE TREK CREW BOOK, STEPHEN KING & CLIVE BARKER: THE ILLUSTRATED GUIDE TO THE MASTERS OF THE MACABRE and HOW TO DRAW ART FOR COMIC BOOKS: LESSONS FROM THE MASTERS. He is the publisher of MIDNIGHT GRAFFITI, in which he has run previously unpublished stories by Stephen King and Harlan Ellison as well as the writer of THE GHOSTBUSTERS for Now Comics. Van Hise resides in San Diego along with his wife, horses and various other animals.

# CALLING, TRACY!

## SIX DECADES OF DICK TRACY

By James Van Hise

PIONEER BOOKS, INC.      LAS VEGAS, NEVADA

# Designed and Edited by Hal Schuster

with design assistance from James R. Martin
cover by David Hasle

**Library of Congress Cataloging-in-Publication Data**
James Van Hise, 1949—
    Calling, Tracy—Six Decades of Dick Tracy

    1.    Calling, Tracy—Six Decades of Dick Tracy (literature)
I. Title

Published by Pioneer Books, Inc., 5715 N. Balsam Rd., Las Vegas, NV, 89130.

First Printing, 1990

*Acknowledgements: Every book owes a debt to many hands besides those of the author. This book would not have been the same without the assistance of Shel Dorf, Lawrence Doucet, Hal Schuster, Peter Sanderson, Eric Hoffman and Jim Harmon. Their generosity is greatly appreciated.*

# CONTENTS!

# A word from the author....

Dick Tracy came into being at a time when the traditional world of mysteries established by such writers as Agatha Christie and Sir Arthur Conan Doyle was undergoing a revolution in American letters as the hard-boiled detective school was coming into its own. What was gaining the upper hand in pulp magazines came down hard in the comic strips when Dick Tracy brought modern detective work to the comics pages, seasoned with sudden doses of violence when the villain was cornered. But being the very visual medium that comics are, Tracy's creator, Chester Gould, introduced villains so bizarre, that they were fascinating to watch even in their pauses between criminal acts. Down through the years, which became decades, Gould continued to infuse Tracy with creativity and surprise. Even though Gould is gone now, his character lives on, capturing the imaginations of new fans, whether with the current incarnation of the character, or by discovering the active movie life he had in the Thirties and Forties. This book deals largely with the latter as it's a period often overlooked and shunted aside in favor of the hundreds of pages of comic strip adventures. But Dick Tracy is a man of many adventures, and some of his most interesting were not in black and white in newspapers, but in black and white on the silver screen.

## —JAMES VAN HISE

# DICK TRACY IN THE COMICS

# DICK

# TRACY

# THROUGH

# THE YEARS

*The year was 1931.*
*The adventure comic strip was*
*coming into its own and a*
*young cartoonist named*
*Chester Gould had an idea. .*

His name was Plainclothes Tracy when young Chester Gould first put pen to paper to create the samples of his new comic strip. The year was 1931 and newspapers hungered for new heroes. The Chicago Tribune encouraged Gould, but then suggested a name change. Since Tracy was a police detective, they wanted to call him "Dick," the street slang for detective in those days. Gould agreed to the name Tracy, and added a form of the word "tracing" as in tracking down criminals. Thus did Dick Tracy start taking form.

What Gould never changed was the character's unflagging honesty and integrity. His virtue proved unshakable no matter the provocation. Tracy constantly exemplified unswerving loyalty in his friendships with his sweetheart, Tess Trueheart (whom Tracy married in 1949), his partner, Pat Patton, and later Sam Catchem.

Another fixture in the strip from its earliest days was an orphan named Junior. The orphan soon took on the name Junior Tracy and Tracy adopted him as his son.

Dick Tracy first appeared in newspapers on Sunday, October 4, 1931. Gould wrote the strip from a plot by Captain Joseph Patterson, head of the Chicago Tribune Syndicate. The daily strip began on Monday, October 12, 1931.

Gould had submitted ideas for strips to Patterson previously, but the publisher felt Tracy had the strongest possibilities. He had Gould prepare a story on the strength of the samples, and told him what the plot should be. His basic plot outline was that Dick Tracy should date a girl whose father owns a delicatessen and keeps his receipts in a cigar box under the bed (not unusual in the wake of the 1929 stock market crash). Criminals rob and kill the old man. Gould took it from there and wrote the strip by himself until his retirement in December 1977.

When Gould first began the strip, the Sunday and the daily featured two different stories. He merged them into one continuous thread beginning May 29, 1932.

Arthur Conan Doyle's classic deductive detective Sherlock Holmes still dominated the detective genre at the time of Tracy's creation. Gould drew his inspiration from American writers, primarily Dashiell Hammett whose grim novels were far removed from Holmes and Watson.

Hammett's style of storytelling was already becoming popular in the pulp magazines of the day. By the late Thirties, when Raymond Chandler came into his own, the style dominated. Hammett's novels, including THE MALTESE FALCON and THE CONTINENTAL OP, set the tone for all that followed.

Gould said, "I made a point of not reading any of the modern detective novels. I was of course a big fan of Sherlock Holmes. I did read and reread the Sherlock Holmes stories. I always found some inspiration in them. The Sherlock Holmes stories weren't like Dick Tracy, but they always had that element of suspense in them. Sir Arthur Conan Doyle is the grandfather of the classic suspense story, any kind of suspense story, in my opinion. I also considered myself a disciple of Edgar Allan Poe. As a kid I had been a fan of the Tom Swift stories, which also were always based on danger and menace."

1931

1936

1965

Gould has denied being directly influenced by Hammett or any of the other writers of the "bloody pulps." Some critics suggest the violent tenor of the times independently influenced Gould, Hammett and other writers. They adopted a philosophy of writing which reflected the dark world portrayed in the newspaper stories of the day.

While the hardboiled detective was the fashion in magazine and book fiction, Gould went in a realistic direction. Dick Tracy used modern techniques of detection so that his stories were actually police procedurals. Although this could have quickly become dry and straightforward, the grim fatalism of the hardboiled detective remained. Violence was an inevitable result of realistic confrontations. Only Gould's simplistic, cartooney style kept the violence from being offensive. Even so, such past scenes as a dead felon with bleeding bullet holes in his head (from October 27, 1952) could never be shown today.

Gould's alma mater, Northwestern University, had a modern crime detection laboratory on its campus. The writer/artist took advantage of it to learn more about criminology. He brought an undertone of realism to his strip, no matter how bizarre his villains might be. Chester Gould even secured the services of Al Valandis, one of the nation's first police artists and a retired police officer.

Gould drew inspiration from the incredible headlines of the day. With mobsters such as Bonnie and Clyde, Al Capone, Baby Face Nelson and Dillinger a fact of life, takeoffs on them did not seem fantastic.

The "crime of the century," the kidnapping of the Lindberg baby, even served as inspiration for a case investigated by Dick Tracy. The comic story presented a happier outcome than the real life tragedy.

It wasn't long before Gould felt that imitating real criminals in his strip wasn't enough. In order to outdo his competitors, he had to go them one better and be more inventive. The result was a gallery of outlandish villains. The most popular of these began appearing in the Forties.

B-B-Eyes first appeared in 1942 as a crook who dealt in bootleg tires. This was World War Two and rubber was scarce. B-B-Eyes had it in for Tracy because the criminal's brother had died at Tracy's hands. In keeping with Gould's penchant for his bad guys meeting bizarre and ironic deaths, B-B-Eyes tried to escape Tracy by leaping on to a garbage scow. Trapped in the garbage by a tire, the ship dumped him with its trash into the sea. B-B-Eyes sank to the bottom.

The same year saw the introduction of Pruneface. Reflecting the times, Pruneface was a saboteur bent on destroying a bomb-sight factory located not far from where he's rented a room. As fate would have it, his landlady is the mother of Tess Trueheart, Tracy's fiance. When he fails due to the intervention of Tess and her mother, Pruneface flees, hampered by a broken leg. His accomplice kidnaps a doctor to set his leg, but Pruneface is so paranoid he refuses to let the physician give him an anesthetic. He insists on remaining wide awake at all times, even when the doctor is setting his bone. Tracy

# Gould Artwork Before Tracy

### EARY CARTOONING BY CHESTER GOULD
(PRIOR TO DICK TRACY)

1,2,3 = SCHOOL YEARBOOK
    CARTOONS (1918-19)
4 = SPORTS CARTOON (1931)
5 = "BUUZZY", AN EARLY (1920's)
    REJECTED STRIP IDEA
6 = GOULD'S ONCE-A-WEEK
    STRIP FOR KING FEATURES
    SYNDICATE (1924)
7 = VARIATION OF #6 FOR RADIO PG.
8,9, = FILLUM FABLES" (1928)

## Two of Tracy's most famous villains first appeared in 1944.

tracks Pruneface down and takes him alive to secure information vital to America's national security. Tracy predicts the hideous villain's future will be a simple one, "Hospital, county jail and electric chair."

Two of Tracy's most famous villains first appeared in 1944. Flattop was a hit man. They were called paid assassins or contract killers in those days. Hired to kill Tracy, he kidnaps the police detective and then contacts his employers, demanding more money to complete the job. When Tracy escapes, the hoodlum flees. Along the way he encounters a new supporting character, Vitamin Flintheart, a has-been actor who constantly pops vitamin pills. Flattop attempts to elude Tracy by hiding aboard a replica antique ship anchored in the harbor. When he leaps overboard to elude Tracy, he becomes trapped in the pilings holding the ship at anchor and drowns.

The Brow, a classic villain and Nazi spy, uses the naive Summer sisters as catspaws. When Tracy captures the two notorious pickpockets and plans to use them as key witnesses against the Brow, the hideous villain has the girls killed. In fleeing Tracy, the Brow encounters a strange woman named Gravel Gertie, yet another character destined to join the regular supporting cast of the strip. Gertie becomes infatuated with the temporarily blinded Brow, whom she nurses in her shack. When the Brow regains his sight and sees Gertie's hideousness, he flees and is found by Tracy. The lovestruck Gertie attempts to help the Brow escape, but Tracy knocks the Nazi through a window where he is impaled on a flagpole!

Other villains in the rogues' gallery are Shakey (1945), Breathless Mahoney (1946) and Mumbles (1947). Still other foes include the offspring of Flattop and the Brow, bizarre foes such as The Blank, The Mole, Half and Half, Blowtop, Torcher, Coffeyhead, Wormy, Measles, Dewdrop, Mousey, Pearshape, Scorpio and Ugly Christine.

The late Forties brought another new supporting character to the strip, Sam Catchem. Created as Tracy's partner, Catchem was Jewish and became as familiar a fixture in the strip as Tracy himself.

Dick Tracy came along at a very fertile time for comic strips. The adventure strip and its larger-than-life heroes were born in 1929, with the appearances of TARZAN and BUCK ROGERS. While new to comics, they had appeared in books and magazines. Gould was one of the first to create an entirely original adventure hero for the strips. Within two years he had half-a-dozen imitators. Gould remarked that while the violence in his strip caused concern at first, his imitators were not at all squeamish about copying it. Earlier complaints were soon forgotten.

Gould's style was crude and cartooney at first, but he refined it. Finally, although still simplistic, it possessed undeniable energy which propelled the story. Once he captured the technique he wanted, Gould maintained it for some forty years until his retirement with the December 11, 1977 Sunday page. Gould had written and drawn Dick Tracy for 46 years, two months and 21 days. Over those years, he won the Reuben Award for "Outstanding Cartoonist of the Year" twice, in 1959 and in 1977.

Comic art historian Maurice Horn describes Gould's work by saying, "Gould's renderings were black, ominous, his line sharp and nervous, the perspective compact, oppressive. His imagery Gould took directly from new photos, complete with sharply-edged contours and flattened backgrounds, photoprints of the city's soul, with its skyscapes, its back alleys, its gaudy neon signs, its grandeur and squalor."

Al Capp, the creator of Li'l Abner and a contemporary of Gould, once paid him a high compliment. Capp said, "To write the continuity of a script is one of the most complicated methods of developing a story, for the author must relate his main script in a series of short episodes — the daily strips — and each one of these short episodes must contain all the elements of a complete story— introduction, climax, conclusion - plus the suspense. Everything I know about comic strip narration I learned not only through my own efforts but from the study of two great masters: Chester Gould and Harold Gray."

Capp parodied Gould's Tracy with a character he created called Fearless Fosdick. He secured Gould's permission before he did the parody. Gould, believing it would be a one-time bit like so many other satires Capp had done, gladly granted his permission. When Fosdick scored a big hit, Capp continued the character for years.

Once DICK TRACY became successful, Gould employed assistants. His first was Dick Moores, who would later take over the GASOLINE ALLEY comic strip. Other assistants Gould employed down through the years include Russell Stamm, Carol Anderson, Jack Ryan, his own brother Ray Gould, Dick Locher and Rick Fletcher. Assistants generally did odd jobs for the artist, which could even include delivering the completed strips to the syndicate, as well as inking backgrounds or doing lettering. Gould wrote the strip himself, pencilled it and almost never let anyone else ink the actual drawings of his Dick Tracy character.

When Gould retired, mystery writer and Tracy fan Max Allan Collins took over the writing chores, while Rick Fletcher took on the art. When Fletcher died of cancer in 1983, former Gould assistant Dick Locher returned to the strip.

Locher draws the strip in a style similar to Gould's, but by no means identical. It is clear the art is not by Gould, primarily in the rendering of faces.

When Collins took over the strip, with Gould's permission he made changes to return to the gritty reality identified with the feature from the Thirties through the Fifties. Collins killed off the Moon Maid in a car bomb explosion.

Trying to keep a jump ahead of everyone, Gould had run riot with science fiction elements in the Sixties. These included the "Space Coupe," an interesting anti-gravity ship capable of flying to the moon, and the inhabitant it brought back, the Moon Maid. In one Sixties episode the Space Coupe was stolen and the body of a man was ejected into space high in orbit over the earth. While purists were unhappy with the Space Coupe and similar sci fi elements, other fans remember them fondly.

Dick Tracy has inspired hundreds of collectible toys and books over the years, including versions of Tracy's famous two-way wrist radio. A science fiction device when introduced decades ago, as technology marched on it was transformed into a two-way wrist TV in the Sixties. The wrist-radio remains one of the most oft-produced Tracy toys. Even people who never followed the comic strip inevitably saw a drawing of Tracy wearing his famous watch and the words "two-way wrist-radio." This was the way Gould always drew Tracy when he used the device, no matter how many times we'd seen Tracy use it before.

Early strips reappeared in such comic books (not collectible themselves) as POPULAR COMICS #1-27 beginning in 1936 and SUPER COMICS #1-115 from 1938 to 1947. Then there was Dell's DICK TRACY MONTHLY #1-24 published from 1948 to 1949 and later picked up by Harvey Comics with issue #25 and continued until #145 in 1961. Recent books reprinting the strips include the lavish THE CELEBRATED CASES OF DICK TRACY as well as the more moderately priced DICK TRACY: AMERICA'S MOST FAMOUS DETECTIVE. Blackthorne Press issued a series of small books reprinting many of Tracy's earliest adventures.

Chester Gould died in May of 1984 at the age of 84. His strip lives on in the hearts and minds of fans of all ages, as well as in newspapers across the country and around the world. It remains one of the few adventure strips to have survived into the 1990's.

# Dick Tracy's Rogues Gallery

STOOGE VILLER
1933

"MOLE"
1941

LITTLEFACE
1941

B-B EYES
1942

PRUNEFACE
1943

MRS. PRUNEFACE
1943

THE BROW
1944

VITAMIN FLINTHEART
1944

FLATTOP SR.
1944

SHAKEY
1945

BREATHLESS MAHONEY
1946

MUMBLES
1947, 1955

SHOULDERS
1948

SKETCH PAREE
1949

# A

# LOOK

# AT

# STORY

# HIGHLIGHTS

*Tracy stories have thrilled readers for over half a century with colorful villains, interesting supporting characters, evocative artwork, clever plots...and, of course, Dick Tracy!*

Dick Tracy made his grand entrance on Sunday, October 4, 1931 in the DETROIT MIRROR. Another Sunday page followed on October 11, but the strip only began to get nationwide exposure when the daily appeared for the first time in the NEW YORK TIMES on Monday, October 12. The first story continuity ran through December 30, 1931. Although THE CELEBRATED CASES OF DICK TRACY (Chelsea House, 1970) ends the first episode on November 13, the story actually continues until December 30. In DICK TRACY: THE THIRTIES—TOMMY GUNS AND HARD TIMES (Chelsea House, 1978) they pick up this story from November 16 and continue it to its proper conclusion. The Sunday pages were not a part of the normal continuity at this time and the two didn't merge until May 29, 1932. The Sunday pages form part of the continuity in the stories and often portray key events otherwise only recapped with a couple of sentences in Monday's daily.

Even in his first appearance, Dick Tracy was not a policeman. He solved a crime in his first Sunday page by having been a witness to a crime and then using his wits to unmask the criminal.

In the daily strip we meet Dick Tracy and Tess Trueheart. We discover that Tracy, although well-dressed, is out of work due to the Great Depression, just as many other Americans were at the time. Dick is visiting Tess at her parents' home in an apartment above the deli they own. In the fourth daily strip Tracy and Tess announce their plans to wed.

Villainy lurks nearby as two hoods, Ribs Mocco and Crutch have been casing the building. They have determined that Mr. Trueheart keeps his money in a wall safe, a practice he began when banks closed during the previous year. The masked men burst in and brutally gun down the elder Trueheart when he tries to stand up to them. He finally reveals the location and combination of the safe with his dying breath to spare his family.

When Tracy tries to intervene, he's pistol whipped and knocked unconscious. The crooks rob the safe and kidnap Tess.

The change in direction of Tracy's life becomes evident on October 21. He stands in the small apartment, eyes heavenward, and vows, "Over the body of your father, Tess, I swear I'll find you and avenge this thing—I swear it."

The next day, the chief of police offers Tracy a job on the Plainclothes Squad, stating, "I think you'd be a big help in finding Tess Trueheart and catching her father's murderer." Without any type of on-stage interview, nothing is revealed of Tracy's life prior to his meeting with Tess at her home. They must be pretty impressed with him, however, as the next day's strip states that Tracy prepares to lead the police dragnet in search of Tess.

The rest of the story is pretty routine. Tracy goes undercover and, purely by happenstance, hooks up with the exact same group of thugs who kidnapped Tess.

When the gang Tracy joins plans a robbery, he alerts the police who trap the thieves inside. The crooks force Tess to drive the getaway car and plan to double-cross Tracy during the robbery. When gang members identify Tracy, a pursuit ensues.

Through luck and skill Tracy escapes with Tess. He then takes her to the hospital where her mother is recovering and Tess learns of the death of her father. The crooks had maintained that he wasn't seriously hurt in order to control her.

At this point the story concludes in THE CELEBRATED CASES OF DICK TRACY. In actuality, it's only at the mid-way point. The gang then plans retribution on Tracy, but an assassination attempt goes awry. Crutch is slain and Ribs Mocco is hospitalized in the attempt.

Tracy tries to interrogate the thug about his boss, Big Boy, but he won't talk. Suddenly the scene shifts to Tracy raiding Big Boy's hide-out. Although it's never revealed, we have to figure either Ribs was convinced to talk or this hide-out is the same place Tess was brought when she was kidnapped.

When Big Boy flees to the home of his moll, Texie Garcia, there's a scene where he has her play a tune on a piano. For some reason Tracy knows that Big Boy can play. No explanation for this knowledge appears. The bit is actually copied from a scene in one of the five sample "Plainclothes Tracy" strips which Chester Gould wrote and drew to sell the concept to the Chicago Tribune Syndicate. These five daily strips never appeared as part of the regular continuity but were printed first in DICK TRACY: THE THIRTIES. They reappeared in DICK TRACY: AMERICA'S MOST FAMOUS DETECTIVE (Citadel Press, 1987).

Although Tracy didn't marry Tess for quite some time, their relationship remained important. With Christmas approaching in the series, Tess tries to get Tracy into the spirit of the season. He's bent on tying up his case when he realizes Texie is about to be murdered by a crook she's been blackmailing.

Big Boy has split town after shooting and wounding Tracy's partner, Pat. The action then shifts to the lawyer Texie calls to bail her out and climaxes with her flight and the suicide of the crooked politician she'd been blackmailing.

In typical soap opera fashion, Tess feels sorry for herself. Tracy is too busy to spend Christmas Eve with her, but he buys her an engagement ring as soon as he wraps up the case. It's an okay story, but not a particularly auspicious beginning for a newspaper strip which is still running fifty-nine years later. The best was yet to come.

Gould's artwork at this time was fairly standard for the day and not particularly individualistic or stylized. A comics page from 1931 offered many strips similarly rendered strips, both humor or "straight" series such as LITTLE ORPHAN ANNIE. Comics had a familiar look to them in those days. Even the earliest weeks of Alex Raymond's FLASH GORDON in 1934 had this look. As Raymond's strips built up a following and the artist honed his craft, he developed his own unique technique. This was as true of Gould as it was of Raymond.

"The Demotion Of Dick Tracy" (December 31, 1931 to February 20, 1932) deals primarily with Tracy's relationship with Tess. When he confides in her the secret plan for a police raid and the raid fails, he believes she told someone else. He and Tess argue and she calls off the engagement, as Tracy won't listen to what she has to say and believes the worst. He becomes so despondent over the breakup that his work suffers and he's demoted to being a beat cop. Tess finally cools down and decides to help Tracy by revealing a plot she overheard discussed in a restaurant. She does so via a note taped to Tracy's apartment door.

Tracy wins back his position as a plainclothes officer and reestablishes their relationship. It's the type of soap opera many readers of comic strips of the time ate up. It is far removed from the bizarre cases Tracy became known for a few years later in the decade.

"The Con Game Of Broadway Bates And Belle" (February 22 to April 9, 1932) introduces a new villain. While not as bizarre as many who followed, he is more colorful than the typical gangsters previously seen in the strip. In his monocle, bowler hat and long nose, Broadway Bates is almost the spitting image of the villain known as The Penguin later introduced into the BATMAN comics in the Forties. Broadway Bates is a con artist who learns of the ten thousand dollars in insurance money Tess Trueheart's mother came into as a result of the murder of Emil Trueheart. While not many people could afford insurance in the Thirties, the comic strip established early on that Emil was a successful store owner, which led to his death. Now the burden of money again raises its head to threaten the Truehearts.

Tracy learns of the scheme to cheat the family. Broadway Bates has him kidnapped by the novel method of having a suitcase full of bricks dropped on Tracy's head from a second story window. It's a wonder it didn't crack his skull open.

Tracy starts to become a more colorful character by this time. While he's held prisoner by the kidnappers, he taunts his tommygun-toting guard by stating, "If the guns were taken away from you muscle-heads, you couldn't think—they're your brains." Tracy isn't as cocky when they torture him by using a blowtorch on his feet to force him to write a ransom note! He succumbs to the torture and writes the note.

## Broadway Bates is almost the spitting image of the The Penguin.

Most heroes stand up to such things, but Tracy is more realistic than most. In real life, I don't think anyone could stand up to having their bare feet fried.

Gould indulges his stylistic bent in this story. The dailies for March 28 through 30 take place at night entirely in silhouette with shading and crosshatching for background. The effective approach captures the bleak mood of the sequence but I have to wonder how well the large black areas reproduced in the newspapers of the day.

The story presents a violent climax when Tracy is freed and attacks his kidnappers. This final confrontation occupies three consecutive dailies.

The crime boss from Tracy's first adventure returns in "Big Boy And The Abduction Of Buddy Waldorf" (April 11 to May 28, 1932) in a story with historic overtones. One of the most infamous crimes of the Thirties was the Lindberg kidnapping case which ended with the world famous aviator's young son being found dead. In this Dick

Tracy story, the two year old son of international financier John H. Waldorf is kidnapped. The Chief of Police observes, "Tracy, this country is in the grip of a plague worse than war! Gangsters are striking at the foundation of America—the home." The police force mobilizes.

An interview with a neighbor of Waldorf's reveals a stranger in the area whom Tracy believes fits the description of Big Boy since the stranger has many gold teeth. Tracy unearths clues which enable him to trace Big Boy to a cruise ship where he discovers the villain with a female accomplice who has a young blond boy with her. When Tracy discovers blond hair dye he realizes that the black-haired Waldorf child is there on the ship.

Tracy can't collar the man very easily as he's identified by Big Boy, captured, tied up and thrown overboard. A passing fishing boat crew finds Tracy. He then transfers to an aircraft carrier and later flies back to the cruise ship before it can reach shore. Tracy captures Big Boy just as the crime kingpin decides the law is closing in and it's time to dispose of the evidence—the child.

Big Boy first pushes his unconscious female accomplice out through the porthole and is about to do the same with the child when Tracy bursts into the room. Tracy rescues the child then has the Captain close the door so he can have a few minutes in private with Big Boy. Tracy takes full advantage of the opportunity, using his fists to repay the man for his crimes.

In an ending fraught with drama, the child's mother is bedridden, lapsing in and out of a coma. She thinks everyone is lying to her when they claim the child has been rescued.

In the May 28 daily, the last two panels are wordless as Tracy appears before the child's parents holding the little boy. In the very last panel, the mother hurls herself out of bed to embrace the son she'd believed lost to her forever. These wordless panels communicate intense feeling.

## The Blank

## was a

## man with

## no face.

The opening of "Alec Penn, Bond Forger" (May 30 through July 30, 1932) forms a brief epilogue to the kidnapping story. Tracy and Tess have dinner with the Waldorfs in a very touching scene. When John Waldorf offers Tracy fifty thousand dollars in securities as a reward, Tracy notices that ten thousand dollars of them are counterfeit.

This leads into a story filled with routine running around climaxing in an interesting sequence. Tracy and Pat Paxton become trapped in a secret room behind a lion's cage. The sequence is suspenseful as they use their wits to prevent the lions from breaking into the room. They're ultimately rescued when Waldorf shows up on the scene, realizes what is happening and shoots the poor caged beasts (the lions, that is).

The story is a bit of a let-down after the more imaginative kidnapping caper which preceded it.

"Blackmailer Of Devil's Island" (August 1 to September 7, 1932) is notable primarily for an unbelievable sequence in which Tracy 'rassles a grizzly. It is the first story in which a villain dies a horrible, violent death in the climax when a dope smuggler and blackmailer perishes in an avalanche of rocks.

The sequence from September 8 to October 12, 1932 marks the first appearance of Junior Tracy. He would quickly become one of the most popular supporting characters in the strip's long continuity.

Junior is a homeless nine-year-old boy being used by a tramp named Steve to steal for him. When Junior steals Pat Paxton's watch and then refuses to break into houses for Steve, the tramp decides to get rid of the boy. He intends to throw him under a train, but Tracy intervenes just in time. Tracy and the orphan forge a strong bond.

It's not long before the nameless boy (Who Steve the tramp only ever called "kid") wants to be known as Dick Tracy, Jr. He wants to move in with Dick.

One night the boy sees Tess's purse lying on a dresser with money in it and his old hobo ways emerge. He steals it and runs until his conscience gets the better of him. He then returns it, restoring Tracy's faith.

When Steve the tramp is released after serving ten days for vagrancy, he tries to kidnap Junior in a comedy of errors. He finally gives up and hops a freight train, but vows to return.

In the following story, "Dan The Squealer and the Science Of Ballistics," Junior goes to work for a man who turns out to be a crook. When Tracy tracks the thug down for a confrontation, the lights in the room go out. When they come back on, Tracy lies unconscious, having been shot. Junior is with him and the only fingerprints on the gun are the boy's.

This leads the police to wonder whether Junior might not have been a setup from the beginning. Junior is heartbroken over what's happened to Tracy, particularly when the police force the boy to live in a detention home.

When Tracy regains consciousness, he insists the boy is innocent. The police aren't so sure. Using ballistics, Tracy proves the bullet the doctors removed from him was not shot from the gun the police

hold as evidence. Before Tracy has Junior freed, the boy breaks out
of the detention home and escapes into the next story. Junior and
Tracy are finally reunited.

They're soon separated again when Steve the tramp hears of a
rich old man searching for his long lost son. Steve kidnaps Junior,
hoping to pass him off as the rich man's son and collect the reward.

It turns out Junior really is the old man's son. His wife had run
off years before when he was a poor prospector, before he finally
struck it rich. Tracy catches up to them but reluctantly leaves Junior
with his real father. Adding to the poignancy is not just Junior's love
of Tracy and his heartache upon leaving him but that the boy's real
father is blind. It's virtually impossible for the reader to resent the
man for coming between Junior and Tracy.

Steve the tramp is captured and sent to prison. When he breaks
out with Stooge Viller, Tracy comes to bring Junior and his father
east to keep them in protective custody until Steve is recaptured.

After a long series of events, Stooge Viller encounters Junior and
his father and is bent on killing the boy to revenge himself on Tracy.
Junior's father is shot while protecting the boy. The old man dies on

August 1, 1933, enabling Junior and Tracy to be reunited under the
most tragic of circumstances.

Although the strip often shows crooks and cops being shot, when
Junior's father is shot, it happens between panels. Only the smoking
gun makes the tragedy clear. Strangely, Stooge Viller actually looks
shocked when he realizes what's happened. The idea that he shot a
blind man was probably meant to be shocking.

Under the daily routine of drawing Tracy, Gould gradually im-
proved his art. It became more slick and polished. By 1933, his ex-
perience on hundreds of strips showed in his developing technique.
He was beginning to develop his fine sense of spotting blacks, an essential talent in black and white comic strips.

**Mama scalds Jerome to death for abandoning her. It marks the end of a match made in Hell.**

Gould didn't employ this technique was in his Sunday pages. There he used fewer dark areas to allow the colors to add dimension to the strip.

Eventually Gould's heightened sense of drama spilled over onto the color page as well.

By 1937, that sense of drama locked firmly in place. Dick Tracy became the first and the best of the newspaper detective strips.

While many villains had come and departed since Dick Tracy joined the plainclothes squad in 1931, the first of his truly weird foes appeared in 1937. Gould was ever ready to innovate and move in new directions in the strip, despite its huge success and prominence in the field of newspaper syndication. Rather than resting on his laurels, Gould forged ahead. He wanted to remain at least one step, if not several, ahead of his competition. On October 5, 1937, Gould began the saga of Frank Redrum, alias "The Blank," which continued through January 6, 1938.

The Blank was a man with no face. This baffles those who meet him. Criminals who have long known him recognize him and call him The Blank. They don't comment on why he wears such a disguise. For most of the story we're not sure it is a disguise, although we wonder how he can see, breathe and talk. This is ultimately explained.

At first the Blank pretends to be a crime-fighter to mask his true motives. When Junior Tracy lies minutes from death by carbon monoxide poisoning after being tied up and shoved under a car with its motor running in a garage, the Blank shows up. He saves Junior and sticks the two men responsible under the car. He then forces the boy to accompany him so that he cannot warn anyone of what's happened until it's too late to save the criminals. The Blank even tries to force Junior to help him bind the men and shove them under the car. Even though the men just tried to kill him, Junior refuses. The Blank releases Junior across town an hour later, knowing that it's too late to help the men in the garage.

The Blank commits gruesome crimes and is soon revealed as a criminal who escaped from prison ten years before. Society has long believed him dead. Now he's come back to gain final revenge on his old gang.

One of his most heinous acts occurs when he kidnaps one of his former gang members. He commandeers a plane and its pilot and pushes his old comrade out of the aircraft at five thousand feet without a parachute. The popularity of the strip was such that this crime was perpetrated on a Sunday page at a time when DICK TRACY often appeared on the front page of color comic sections. Bombs away!

Dick Tracy solved crimes using modern police methods even in the Thirties. In this story he demonstrates the wet film process of lifting a bloody hand print in order to get The Blank's fingerprints as a photograph. Then Tracy has to go through the laborious process of matching the fingerprints to those in his files. This is the way it was done until recently when fingerprint matching was computerized.

**A circus performer rescues Tracy in a daring display of athletic grace.**

As the police begin to close in and the Blank tracks down his last victim, he becomes more desperate. He even blows up the fishing boat his victim is on while Tracy and Pat Paxton are aboard. Although the boat disintegrates into kindling, Tracy and Pat survive and the intended victim remains unconscious and intact. This infuriates the Blank so much he captures Tracy and the unconscious man, takes them below decks on another boat and puts them in a decompression chamber. Then he tries to kill them with compressed air in a very convincing death trap.

Tracy escapes through the help of Pat Paxton, who captures the Blank on his own. With the help of Tracy's hand signals, Pat decompresses the chamber to prevent Tracy from suffering the bends by opening the door too soon.

The Blank unmasks on January 6, 1938. It's revealed he wore a piece of flesh colored cheesecloth glued over his face, a concept refined years later when Steve Ditko created The Question in comic books of the Sixties. One wonders as to Chester Gould's inspiration. This is surely one of the weirdest villains in the Dick Tracy canon, a definite harbinger of things to come.

The tale of "Jerome Trohs and Mamma" (April 22 to July 13, 1940) keeps with Gould's periodic use of a man and woman criminal team. They were seldom cut from the same cloth. In this case Jerome was a midget (a term no longer in vogue) and his girlfriend, known only as Mamma, is a tall, obese woman. They're both ruthless and sadistic.

Jerome poses as an imprisoned gangsters' attorney. He brings his St. Bernard in with him and the dog pokes its head into the cell so that the thug can get the gun hidden in the animal's mouth.

Since the gun isn't loaded, the felon dies in his jailbreak attempt, just as Jerome planned. Meanwhile, Jerome escapes by fleeing on the back of the dog.

Jerome establishes his leadership by having his gang kidnap Tracy so they can torture him and cripple his gun hand. This causes Tracy to wear a cast for the rest of the story.

Mamma constantly eats candy. When the police track her through her candy and Pat Paxton cuffs her to place her under arrest, she attacks him and whirls him around until the handcuffs break. Pat is hurled through a plate glass window.

She further displays her brutality when she's out walking her dog. When it attacks Oscar, a little dog being walked by Junior Tracy, she lets the attack proceed. When the police finally track her down again, they're ready. Four of them take her into custody after two of them tackle her and wrestle her to the ground.

She later breaks out of jail and tracks down Jerome, who fled when she was captured. Tracy has to subdue her by himself in a particularly violent contest after she scalds Jerome to death for abandoning her. It marks the end of a match made in Hell.

Gould's art is slick and tight by this time. While his work would never be mistaken for that of Hal Foster or Alex Raymond, it effectively illustrates the cartoon melodrama. The art served the story. Gould's strength as an artist rested in his rendering of expressive fa-

*The Mole demands Duke's entire haul as payment. Duke is forced to agree, but when he tries to escape that night, the Mole catches and strangles the hood.*

cial characterizations. They perfectly captured the intense emotions of crime drama.

Little Face Finny (July 14 to September 15, 1941) is another weird addition to the Rogues Gallery. He has a particularly high forehead and a face scrunched down into half the area it should normally occupy. One wonders whether Gould is saying genetic defects launch one on the road to crime.

From time to time Gould tells a story of a villain where things start going downhill for him and just keep getting worse. The tale of Little Face is just such a case.

The story opens with Little Face sending in two hoods disguised as women to rub out a gang member who's in the hospital preparing to talk to the police. They silence the man with a blast from a tommygun. Then to further emphasize the viciousness of the gangster, he punishes one of his gang for stupidity by setting his coat on fire and letting it burn. The thug's face becomes so badly burned he has to be taken to medical attention. This begins a chain of events which draws Dick Tracy into the case.

Tracy tries to spy on the office occupied by Little Face using a window washer's scaffolding, but nearly dies when he's spotted and the rope is cut. A circus performer rescues Tracy in a daring display of athletic grace.

Little Face tries to commandeer a taxi but gets caught in the back with his head sticking out until he uses his feet to attack the driver. The driver had tried to transport the felon to the police. Little Face's actions cause the cab to crash into a lake and he barely escapes alive.

He makes the mistake of hiding in a cold storage locker and nearly dies, contracting such severe frostbite that his ears have to be amputated.

Tracy tracks him down, and when gang members carry a rolled up rug out to a truck, Tracy knows Little Face must be wrapped up inside. To prove his theory he tosses a box filled with bees into the truck, forcing Little Face to scramble out and into the waiting arms of the law.

The sequence in which Little Face is treated by the doctor is pretty grotesque. Although Gould only suggests the frostbite by shading on the gangster's face, the story makes it clear the man is suffering; the skin on his face and hands is turning black. Because Gould's art rendered reality without filtering it through the romantic sensibilities found in FLASH GORDON or MANDRAKE THE MAGICIAN, such harsh scenes contained more impact.

In TARZAN and PRINCE VALIANT, people were killed or wounded tastefully. In DICK TRACY, the characters suffered pain we could believe because Gould rendered a contemporary reality on its own terms. While the artwork seems simplistic compared to current popular styles, it presented an unvarnished and uncompromising truth.

The story of The Mole (September 17 to December 25, 1941) is a story which goes in many directions, not introducing the main character until halfway through.

The story opens with a man getting out of prison after seven years. When it's revealed this man was formerly known as Steve the Tramp, we recall the 1934 story. This formerly brutal character first appeared in the same strip that launched Junior Tracy. Steve is completely reformed now.

Strangely, even though Gould states seven years have passed for Steve in prison, Junior hasn't aged seven years. He was ten when he last saw Steve and he's certainly not seventeen at this point, but seemingly twelve. Only bad guys suffer the ravages of age in comic strips.

The first half of the story concerns a thief named Duke. He keeps slipping up, and finally after stealing two thousand dollars, goes to a junk yard where he contacts a man known only as the Mole. The Mole has a hide-out below an abandoned steam boiler. When Duke seeks sanctuary there, the Mole demands Duke's entire haul as payment. Duke is forced to agree, but when he tries to escape that night, the Mole catches and strangles the hood for offending his hospitality.

The Mole looks as most such characters in comic strips have looked over the years. He has a face with a huge nose that dominates his features and seems to merge with his forehead. His face is clearly rodent-like and living underground for so many years seems to have pushed him over the edge.

The Mole is exposed when Tracy searches the area after Duke's body is found in a sewer. The early winter snow is dumped by snowplows into the junkyard, causing the hide-out to cave in.

The Mole manages to dig his way out, emerging from the ground not unlike his namesake and into the waiting arms of the law. In a slightly odd ending, Gould made a nod to the Christmas season, and the last we see of the Mole he's in jail getting a Christmas present!

The miscreant known as B.B. Eyes first appeared in a sequence running from January 27 to April 18, 1942. He doesn't have a season of peace on earth and goodwill towards men to save him from an untimely resolution. Rather it is a saga of grim retribution.

Tracy is captured and imprisoned twice. Laid up with a broken leg, B.B. Eyes kidnaps Tracy. Unlike in real life, Tracy keeps running into criminals who don't just shoot him, but set up elaborate death traps and then walk away expecting him to die.

**The villain known as 88 Keyes is one of those slick, good-looking types who thinks he's smarter than everyone**

The first trap places Tracy and a young woman who owns a nightclub formerly the property of B.B. Eyes dead brother in a basement next to a boiler. It is fired up so that the wired down safety valve will allow it to explode. After B.B. Eyes and his gang leave, the pair are unbound by the woman's mother. She saw Tracy abducted and followed the car.

Later, when they notice the new tires on B.B. Eyes car, they follow that lead. New tires were rare during wartime as rubber was used for the war effort overseas.

Officer O'Malley offers to follow the lead Tracy discovers. It's actually a setup and O'Malley is later found dead in the stack of tires Tracy had arranged to buy from the crooks.

The second time B.B. Eyes captures Tracy, he seals him and Pat Paxton in a tube of solid paraffin (wax) from the chest down. He then leaves them. This time Tracy uses his wits to escape. He's able to tip himself over and roll up to the furnace to soften the paraffin imprisoning him.

When B.B. Eyes returns to check on his prisoners, they capture him and take his gun. While he's being transported to jail, the handcuffed B.B. Eyes leaps from the back of Tracy's car while they're crossing a bridge. He lands, not in the river below, but in the back of a passing garbage barge. Tracy has the Coast Guard run him out to the barge, but it dumps its load before he can reach it.

B.B. Eye's struggles helplessly in the muck and garbage. He is dragged to the river bottom. An old tire imprisons him helplessly until he drowns.

The villain known as 88 Keyes (April 15 to July 14, 1943) is one of those slick, good-looking types who thinks he's smarter than everyone else but soon outsmarts himself. When he engineers the murder of a wealthy man at the behest of the man's wife, suspicion quickly falls on her since they'd only been married two weeks. Much is made of the two hundred thousand dollar insurance policy. Nothing is said about the value of his estate.

88 Keyes betrays one person after another in this story. When his female accomplice discovers he's planning to run away with the wealthy widow, he kills his accomplice. He then puts her body in a piano, where it is soon discovered by Tracy.

By this time 88 Keyes has left with the widow in her car right after obtaining the insurance money in cash. He soon leaves her in her car asleep so that a train will nail it at a railroad crossing. This is just his latest mistake. He soon discovers the police are onto him and has to run.

88 Keyes keeps using and taking advantage of people, then betraying them when it's to his advantage. In a strange touch, an adolescent girl falls for 88 Keyes and runs off with him. Because of his treatment of his previous accomplices, we expect him to ice her at any moment. Instead she turns on him and deliberately wrecks their car when she realizes he's a criminal after he robs a store. This brings Tracy hot on his heels.

The musician finally meets his end when he hides in a shack. Tracy uses a machine gun to insure the fugitive won't surprise him.

**DICK TRACY**

**DICK TRACY**

**DICK TRACY**

**DICK TRACY**

## It begins innocently enough with Tracy arresting the Summer Sisters.

This was one of the most complicated stories written by Gould up to that time. The series of events logically meshes together. The daily serial form produces a story of complexity more often found in a novel. While in many stories Tracy and the villain have equal time, 88 Keyes is clearly the main character in this adventure. Tracy is his dogged adversary, picking up the pieces of the puzzle the felon leaves.

Towards the end, however, the two hundred thousand dollars 88 Keyes supposedly stole from Mrs. Helmet before killing her isn't mentioned. He doesn't use it to facilitate his escape. It seems to be a loose end left untied.

Flattop (December 21 to March 24, 1944) presents a new wrinkle in Tracy's life. He is a hitman brought in from out of town specifically to kill Dick Tracy.

Tracy's investigations are taking him too close to uncovering the activities of a gang and so they hire Flattop to get rid of the police detective. Why they think this would end the investigation (policemen do keep files, after all) isn't made clear.

Flattop captures Tracy right off and is on the verge of shooting him in the back of the head when he gets a better idea. He holds his employers up for more money, demanding fifty thousand dollars for Tracy. They debate the demand and finally give in.

In the meantime, Tracy alerts the police, who move in when the fight between Tracy and Flattop begins. Tracy guns down his guards while the hitman makes tracks. Flattop is finally captured in a violent shoot-out with police and lives to tell the tale, albeit in police custody.

In a grimly realistic sequence, Flattop befriends a young man who tries to pick his pocket and is taken to a rooming house where he can hide out. The young man soon recognizes the fugitive from newspaper photos and starts shaking down Flattop for fifty dollars at a time. The shakedowns end when the boy buys a pair of ice skates and uses them on a pond with thin ice. Scenes of the silhouette of the boy's body under the ice are creepy and effective.

This story introduces Vitamin Flintheart. The exaggerated character is supposed to be an aging Shakespearean actor who's rather foolish and absent minded. The comic persona clashes with the style of melodrama employed in the strip.

The strange tale of the gangster known as The Brow begins on May 22 and runs through September 23, 1944. It begins innocently enough with Tracy arresting the Summer Sisters, two young women who are twins as well as pickpockets. Tracy puts them on a train out of the city, but they escape and meet up with the Brow. He pays them to work for him. It's forced duty as he has one sit with her leg in a spike machine which will close on her if the other doesn't return from her errand in time.

They quickly find a way to rebel. One of them gets a gun and starts shooting the Brow's men. The twins escape, leaving the Brow unconscious with his head and shoulder in the activated spike machine.

The Brow finally comes to and escapes with gory results. He's now wanted by the police.

Tracy attempts to hold the Summer sisters in protective custody, but they won't hear of it. No sooner do the two women leave police headquarters than the Brow, who's been waiting and plotting his revenge, follows. The Brow and his accomplice force the cab off a bridge into a river. The police officer in the cab escapes, but the Summer sisters slowly drown.

Gould spares few details of their final moments, even showing the bodies of the two women and the cab driver in the car at the river bottom.

The Brow and his accomplice, Doc, split up. Doc flees the police but crashes his car into a steel bridge railing. Tracy corners the Brow in a theater. The Brow, out of bullets, hurls an old lightning rod which hits Tracy in the shoulder, deflecting his aim. The gangster then escapes the police.

Blinded by a bleeding head wound, the Brow is found and taken in by Gravel Gertie. She nurses him back to health and hides him from the police.

Gravel Gertie is another exaggerated cartoon of a character who, when she sees the Brow with his blood-spattered face lying in a car, exclaims, "Ah! A Man!" She falls in love with the Brow, but when he gets well enough to remove the bandages from his eyes and sees what she looks like, he flees. Fleeing, he knocks over an oil lamp and burns down her shack.

The Brow is taken alive along with Gravel Gertie. She later marries an even more unpleasant character, B.O. Plenty.

The story of the gangster Mumbles (October 16 to December 10, 1947) is pretty routine and not one of Gould's better Tracy adventures.

Mumbles uses a music quartet he's organized to get into parties given by the wealthy and rob the people who attend. His former girlfriend, Kiss Andtel, quits the group as the lead singer and goes to the police when she realizes that she's being used.

Mumbles forces her to help him on another gig and then flees the country. Tracy tracks them down when Mumbles sets a dynamite bomb to blow up his confederates. Mumbles escapes on a life raft just before Tracy boards the boat. The detective finds the dynamite just in time and throws it overboard, capturing the gang, except for Mumbles.

Mumbles is already far from shore on a life raft. No one ever learns what happens to him as he punctures the raft and drowns.

While Mumbles is an oddball villain, the story just isn't up to par.

Gould continued to write and draw Tracy for many years. While the Fifties offered routine melodramas and pedestrian villains, one bright spot was the introduction of policewoman Lizz on January 1, 1955. She would go from a policewoman in training to Tracy's partner and one of the most fully realized female characters in comic strips. She was portrayed as self-reliant at a time when most female characters in comics were defined only by their relationship to the male characters.

Her first case turned out to be solving the murder of her own sister. Gould didn't skimp on the melodrama.

In 1962, with interest high in America's youthful space program, Chester Gould plunged Dick Tracy into his own space race. He updated the technology of the strip into the realm of science fiction. Diet Smith's development of the Space Coupe provided an imaginative looking anti-gravity aircraft capable of flying from the earth to the moon. Some fans felt the strip went too far. However, Space Coupe stories were surrounded by the type of crime detection cases familiar to fans of the series. If anything, Diet Smith's Space Coupe was Gould's way of breathing new life into a strip he'd been writing and drawing for thirty years.

Gould should be admired for daring new things. After all, most thirty year old strips become unchanging, stagnant. Rereading strips from Gould's four decades on the series, the Space Coupe stories seem slick and interesting as though they'd been done in the Eighties. They don't date but stand up as well as the classic stories of the Thirties and Forties.

An artist should never be expected to keep repeating himself. The Space Coupe stories are highly entertaining and stand out against the more routine cops and robbers Tracy adventures.

In 1977, Chester Gould retired. The Dick Tracy strip was taken over by mystery writer Max Allan Collins and artist Rick Fletcher. When Fletcher (a long time assistant of Gould's) died, another Gould assistant, Dick Locher, stepped in. While the strip has continued to be as contemporary as ever, Max Collins concocted a clever storyline in 1985 called "Tracy's Wartime Memories" which ran from March 18 to September 4, 1985. Most of the story consists of an untold tale of Tracy's from World War Two which included Flattop, Shaky, Pruneface and Mrs. Pruneface. It tells the tale of a new explosive called Xylon invented by an eccentric scientist.

## Max Collins concocted a clever storyline called "Tracy's Wartime Memories."

The scientist is kidnapped for his secret by Flattop after Shaky fails in stealing a copy of the formula. Both Shaky and Flattop work for a mysterious Nazi saboteur referred to only as "the Boche" until he's revealed as Pruneface.

Since the official Pruneface story in the Forties clearly established him as a Nazi agent, this fits perfectly. The best part of the story is the last third in which Pruneface forces the scientist to build Xylon bombs. Even Junior Tracy gets involved in the action. Locher captures the look of Gould's art quite well. Collins' writing is very much in the mold of Gould's World War Two Tracy stories.

Although told in flashback, the story's conclusion takes place in the present day when Tracy and a reporter confront a woman in Washington, D.C. The woman was part of the action in the early Forties. Interestingly, she appears to be forty years older while Tracy never ages.

Max Allan Collins continues to write the adventures of Dick Tracy to this day.

Dick Locher · Max Collins

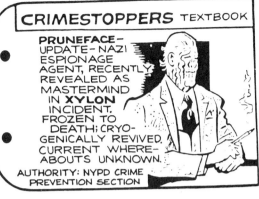

CRIMESTOPPERS TEXTBOOK

PRUNEFACE— UPDATE— NAZI ESPIONAGE AGENT, RECENTLY REVEALED AS MASTERMIND IN **XYLON** INCIDENT. FROZEN TO DEATH; CRYO-GENICALLY REVIVED, CURRENT WHERE-ABOUTS UNKNOWN.

AUTHORITY: NYPD CRIME PREVENTION SECTION

DETECTIVE TRACY— PLEASE WAIT! I HAVE SEVERAL MORE **QUESTIONS** TO ASK—

WENDY, I'VE SAID ALL I HAVE TO SAY ABOUT NORMAL JONES.

"THIS QUESTION CONCERNS A **DIFFERENT** JONES," WENDY SAYS.

3·18

MY QUESTIONS CONCERN **FLATTOP** JONES—

HE'S NO RELATION TO NORMAL, WENDY—

THIS MAY COME AS A **SHOCK** TO THE PRESS, BUT NOT **EVERYBODY** NAMED JONES IS RELATED.

"AND BESIDES—FLATTOP HAS BEEN **DEAD** A LONG, LONG TIME..."

3·19

FLATTOP IS DEAD, BURIED, AND **ANCIENT HISTORY**, WENDY— HARDLY NEWS-WORTHY—

TRUE— BUT, IN A SENSE, HE'S COME **BACK TO LIFE**—

WHAT DO YOU MEAN?

I'LL TELL YOU TOMOR-ROW MORNING, IN MY OFFICE, IF YOU'RE INTERESTED.

3·20

# CHESTER GOULD

## in his own words

*Clhester Gould created and wrote stories of the most popular detective in America for decades*

"Without a doubt, it was this era that planted the idea of DICK TRACY in my head," said Gould, recalling Chicago in the brawling, roaring Twenties. "The revelations of fixed juries, crooked judges, bribery of public officials and cops who looked the other way showed the crying need for a strong representative of law and order who would take an eye for an eye and a tooth for a tooth. Tracy was that man." The creator of Dick Tracy recalled this turbulent time in his introduction to DICK TRACY: THE THIRTIES (Chelsea House, 1978).

Gould further described the influence of his times on his work when he said, "While I was not setting the world on fire, I was still doing an occasional comic strip and working with reporters on special pieces that put me close to the action. There was plenty of that in the Twenties, sparked by the Beer Barons who were constantly warring with each other in a cacophony of machine guns. Though the average law-abiding citizen was more or less insulated from this unpleasant business, it was being abetted and supported by those who patronized the illegal speak."

In an interview conducted by Shel Dorf on July 17, 1978, Chester Gould elaborated on the philosophy that helped him shape the character of Dick Tracy, "I came from Oklahoma where justice was quick and severe when they caught a red-handed culprit. I would read in the papers about a continuance and another continuance and then the judge finds a flaw in the indictment or something. I used to say to myself, 'They know this fellow's a crook. They know that he did this. They know that he is dangerous. Why don't they take him out and shoot him?' That's the way my mind works. I'm putting it crudely, but that was the motivation back of it. In other words, red tape kept these guys from going to jail."

Gould elaborated on this and put it into perspective by stating, "Not for one minute would Tracy be found convicting or mentally censoring a person who has nothing to do with the evil of the situation. His predominant pressure is always to be right. Rather than be right, he will give a little bit at the risk of further complications, rather than get in bad with the people he is trying to help. I think the police will tell you that one of the worst crimes in the world is convicting an innocent person. Of course, that has been terribly overplayed in this permissive age. There are not too many innocent persons in our area of crime prevention that go to jail today. There are too many scientific tests that they can put them through to prove their convictions."

In an interview with Gould published in THE CELEBRATED CASES OF DICK TRACY (Chelsea House, 1970), he elaborated. He said, "What was taking place then was the last stage, you might say, of big-time gangsterism in Chicago. I had submitted numerous ideas to the Tribune and to Captain Joe Patterson of the Tribune syndicate from 1921 until 1931 on various subjects. I found that none of them quite clicked. Then it suddenly dawned on me that perhaps we ought to have a detective in this country that would hunt these fellows up and shoot 'em down. So I developed this character called Plainclothes Tracy.

"Like all things new, it took a couple of months to catch on. Then it grew like wildfire. The salesmen would call me up and say, 'We got two new orders this morning.' There would be two or three orders a day for many, many days. However, from the very beginning I would receive letters saying what a 'horrible' strip I was doing. Now I am used to it and take it with a grain of salt. They don't annoy me one whit any more. The odd thing about them, however, is that they would often describe in detail the 'horrible things.' I figured that they were the types who couldn't wait until the next day to see how a particular thing turned out."

In "Dick Tracy And I," published in 1987 in AMERICA'S MOST FAMOUS DETECTIVE (Citadel Press), Gould defended the presence of violence in the strip. He stated, "Of necessity, gunplay is part of the Dick Tracy strip, and was from the very beginning. That's natural. The law is always armed. Back in 1931 no cartoon had ever shown a detective character fighting it out face to face with crooks via the hot lead route. This detail brought certain expressions of misgiving from newspapers that were prospective Tracy customers. However, within two years this sentiment had faded to the point where six other strips of a similar pattern were on the market and the gunplay bogey had faded into thin air."

Regarding his personal view of the character and the series as a whole, the writer/artist stated, "For me, Dick Tracy has been one continuous detective story. I don't break it down into different periods as many of my fans do. Also I made a point of not reading any of the modern detective novels. I was of course a big fan of Sherlock Holmes. And I did read and reread the Sherlock Holmes stories. I always found some inspiration in them. The Sherlock Holmes stories weren't like Dick Tracy but they always had that element of suspense in them. Sir Arthur Conan Doyle is the grandfather of the

classic suspense story, any kind of true suspense story, in my opinion. I also consider myself a disciple of Edgar Allan Poe. As a kid I had been a fan of the Tom Swift stories, which also were always based on danger and menace.

"I'm often asked where I got the idea for Tracy's face, the square chin and hook nose. Well, in drawing the character, it had been my idea to picture him as a modern Sherlock Holmes, if Holmes were a young man living today, dressed as a modern G-man and bearing the traditional characteristics."

Gould wrote and drew DICK TRACY for over 46 years. While he had art assistants in his later years on the strip, he stuck pretty much to the same creative schedule for all those years.

"My schedule on Dick Tracy was pleasantly rigid and I liked it that way. I did most of my writing on Friday and Monday, did a Sunday on Tuesday, then two or three dailies on Wednesday and three more on Thursday. Sometimes I'd spend time on Friday checking on the mistakes I made earlier in the week. I remember drawing a Sunday page that showed a hoodlum standing in the background, in a doorway, all through the page. Not until the strip got into print did anyone notice that this guy had on four different hats as he stood in that doorway. I found if you can keep to a schedule, you can make yourself available when needed to your family.

"The strip was drawn on 3-ply Strathmore and I used a Gillot 290 pen point. The 290 is more flexible than the 170 pen point which I know many cartoonists use. However, I always wanted to get a swing to my line. I did a lot of brush work and used a Windsor-Newton #4 brush. To me it seemed not too heavy and not too fine.

"Underneath the ink, of course, was some very detailed pencilling with a medium weight pencil that was hard

**DICK TRACY ALWAYS GETS HIS MAN**

Drawn for National Safety Council by Chester Gould

Courtesy, Chicago Tribune — N.Y. News Syndicate

## Public service ad for Farm Safety Week.

enough not to make an impossible smudge from contact with my hand. I also preferred to use a long red eraser called a Pink Lady rather than art gum erasers, which I used just to clean up the whole strip after I'd finished with it. I liked how the Pink Lady would let me get into small areas to change details. Higgins black ink was also what I preferred.

"With my stories I always tried to have two high points per week. Usually one appeared in the dailies between Thursday and Saturday and the final high point would appear in the Sunday. One thing I did that I think was helpful and kept readership was to try to have at least one panel in every daily that the readers felt they had to investigate; something that would appeal to the eye

for just a second so they would take a second look. Often I would use a detail of an everyday object that fitted into the story to contrast with, say, Tracy's profile in the panel before. Then you might jump off to a long shot to move the reader's eye into a completely different perspective.

"I liked to show the latest architecture in the strip to create what some have referred to as 'urban landscapes.' As part of this I got on to a system of drawing inverted V's and totally simplified the process."

Gould felt that layout was just as important in a comic strip as it is in an advertisement, "You have to grab the reader's attention and that's what I tried to do with my layouts. I gave my solid black areas a lot of thought. They were no accident. The black areas were used to direct the reader's eye; you might say they acted as arrows."

Gould explained the writing technique he followed for forty years. He said, "It may shock fans of Dick Tracy, but while I was working on the strip I actually tried to block out of my mind the past villains that I created. That way you can concentrate your creative energy on thinking up new things. I think the best story in the world is one where the writer doesn't know how it's going to end when he starts it. I used to deliberately get Dick Tracy into impossible situations. Then I'd let the drama of the situation simmer for a week. I'd use this as a challenge to myself. If you do things the easy way you get a nothing as a result. That's why I like to write my stories only a week at a time and then draw them, rather than planning weeks in advance."

Chester Gould's DICK TRACY had been around since 1931. In the minds of some, it represented a style of thinking and drawing more relevant to the Thirties than the Eighties. Gould himself was not hesitant in criticizing what he regarded as the decline of the American comic strip both in importance and in creativity, "Without being critical of my peers and cartoonists who are personal friends, I think I can say that this trying to please everybody, the public as a whole, gives you a strip with nothing in it. And I think the general trend to insipidness has lost readers.

"In my estimation, television and a Liberal view on comic strips by editors has delegated all the controversy and conviction to the news end of the business and to columnists, the editorial side. That side has lots of character, but they don't want to be bothered with comic strips. The result is that they've castrated most comic strips from any convictions and turned out a bunch of milk-sop strips. In contrast, the old newspaper kings that built publishing empires in this country were people of conviction."

In THE CELEBRATED CASES OF DICK TRACY, Gould discussed other subjects, including the approach he took to presenting crime and the way he viewed his villains and criminals in general, "I wanted my villains to stand out definitely so that there would be no mistake who the villain was. We were trying very hard to fight the headlines, which were pretty sensational. In the case of Flattop, that very name was taken from the airplane carrier of the day. I think the war was a time when that stuff came easily because so much was suggested by events and there was a very great need for furnishing relief from the damn headlines. I once received a letter from a person asking, 'Why do you make your criminals so ugly?' I never looked at them as being ugly, but I'll tell you this. I think the ugliest thing in the world is the face of a man who has killed seven nurses—or who has kidnapped a child. His face to me is ugly. Or a man who has raped an old lady or young girl and robber her of $3.40. I think this is an ugly man. I think our whole criminal problem has gotten bigger. I think the little innocent street gangs are now using the tactics

employed by the Capones and their hoodlums years ago. I think that through certain court decisions the police have definitely been hamstrung, and I think there has been a psychology that has predominated in the last 20 years that has contributed to permissiveness. It's a complicated thing."

Gould's support of the law enforcement community was strong and public right from the beginning of the Dick Tracy strip, "I have in my home no less than a dozen citations and awards from police departments. I also had the privilege of spending some time with J. Edgar Hoover in the mid-30's."

Gould had fun with the idea of having Dick Tracy, a police officer, living in a house which would have seemingly been impossible for him to afford. Gould anticipated that reaction and played off it deliberately, "Part of the success of my strip is that I have a slogan: 'Bait your enemies and cater to your friends.' I baited. That subject was very hot at the time. There had been some expose' in Chicago about policemen living in 20-room houses and all this. So I thought, 'Gee, this is great, that will cause more damn talk. I'll

*Public service ad for President's Committee on Employment of the Handi- capped*

DICK TRACY SUGGESTS:

HIRE THE HANDICAPPED.

YOU'LL BE GLAD!

CHESTER GOULD

The President's Committee on Employment of the Handicapped, Washington, D.C. 20210

41

have Tracy end up with a tremendous, big house.' There was a period in the 40's, while the war was on, and there were many big homes being given up. I was offered a huge house built around 1920, a home that today would cost you $100,000. In 1943 it was offered to me at $5,000. Many of these old tycoons had passed on. The war came. The boys did this and the other thing, and there stood an old house. To put it in even remotely good condition required only from $5,000 to $10,000. We explained that in the strip—Dick explained it. He said, 'I was offered this house.' He said he paid $4,200—something like that. It had been an old mansion and he jazzed the thing up."

The house was designed in the mold of the architecture of Frank Lloyd Wright by Gould's daughter, who had taken interior design at college.

Gould continued, "It was a helluva buy and a fine looking place, but it needed fixing up. So eventually he had a $50,000 house there, for about $10,000." Interestingly, years later Gould had Tracy's house destroyed by fire in a very dramatic sequence.

In the Sixties, when Gould introduced the Space Coupe, the Moon Maid and other imaginative concepts to DICK TRACY, he was criticized for turning it into a science fiction strip. Gould always hotly denied the charge, "Under no conditions did I consider this science fiction. I considered it a ramification of the potential that we are most definitely going to have to face as we explore space. We haven't scratched the surface yet. For one thing, we have got to get rid of this horse-and-buggy rocket. This thing is perhaps the biggest deterrent to real space exploration that we'll ever have. Will it go to the moon? Yes, of course. Here is a thing that involves such complications, such favorable conditions, such breathtakingly narrow margins of safety, that it must be thrown out of permanent space exploration. We have

to get speed into our space transportation. The idea of taking days to go to the moon almost prohibits the practical use of the whole mission. We're going to have stations on the moon exactly like Diet Smith had them. They will be built of material that will withstand the extreme cold and heat. They will be perhaps 90 per cent underground. We will have colonies up there. I think there are things on the moon that will make it practical to be stationed there. You can be sure, just as sure as we sit here, that we're going to have to protect what we are going to find up there. It's going to be exactly like it was when the New World was explored. Everything is going to be pirated away from the weaklings. There is going to be a very definite need to exercise power.

"I was imaginative in producing people that lived there, however. I have not been completely cleared of the thought that there still may be inhabitants underground, or somewhere where they can live, such as down in a deep ravine, a place like Moon Valley. I am sure that moon travel is here to stay and that we are going to have to get away from rockets, either through magnetic attraction or through some sort of atomic propulsion that has endless power at its command—something that is manageable. Something that won't keep the Army and the Navy and fifty thousand technicians with their fingers crossed, hoping the rocket touches ground."

Gould did not hesitate to voice the opinion that his work on Dick Tracy has had a profound influence on those who followed him, "Yes, but please excuse me if I seem to be a little biased. I feel that Dick Tracy has set a pattern for much of the very excellent entertainment in crime detection and police work. I think the strip has definitely been a tremendous influence in the lives of the writers who have worked in these media."

# MAX ALLAN COLLINS

## in the master's footsteps

*When
Chester Gould
retired from
the strip
he created,
they turned to
successful crime
novelist and
Dick Tracy fan
Max Allan Collins.*

Collins first contact with Dick Tracy came when he was only eight. Collins recalls, "It was a key event in my life. It had a lot to do with my getting into the arts as a profession."

Collins had sent a letter to the creator, Chester Gould. Collins continues, "Actually my mother wrote the letter. I was sitting around the house, drawing pictures of Dick Tracy, and she scooped them up and sent some of them to Chester Gould. She told him I had a birthday coming up. So, on my eighth birthday—actually, it was a couple days after my eighth birthday—I received in the mail this letter from Chester Gould, wishing me a happy birthday. It was an elaborate drawing of Dick Tracy saying hello to me, with Tracy telling me that I drew his picture better than any other kid my age in the country. It was just a wonderful letter. In fact, I carried it around with me for *months* (laughs) and I still have it, framed, in my office at home.

Collins mother played a role in his early interest in the very violent strip. "Well, my mother introduced me to it," Collins admits. "She had followed the strip when she was a young woman.

"I liked comic books, particularly *SUPERMAN* and *DONALD DUCK*. In fact, some were read to me because I was attracted to comic books before I could even read. My mother had to read them to me and guide me through

them, so she picked something that she could stand to read herself. She picked *DICK TRACY*. What attracted me was the violence and excitement of the stories.

"I remember very vividly the first couple of covers that I saw, one of which showed bullets flying through the bad guys' brains. These were the Harvey comic books. It was not the strip. It was not in our local paper.

"I still have that comic book. If I had it in front of me, I'd give you a more accurate description, but it had a bright red cover. Tracy and Sam Catchem were on the wharf, shooting some bad guys who were getting ready to dump one of their fellow members into the water. They had him tied up between a couple of iron pilings. It was an elaborate kind of cement overshoe technique.

"The other issue I remember very, very vividly is the Model story. It is either the first or second story that I ever read. That's my favorite *DICK TRACY* story. It's quite an atypical *DICK TRACY* story, because it was the story in which Gould brought Junior up to adolescence. For twenty-some years, Junior had been a little kid in short pants, and the head of the Crimestoppers. After all that time, Gould finally brought him up into puberty. That story is about his first love. Junior tries to elope with the girl Model, who is a little bit older than he is. She genuinely loves him; but, unbeknownst to Junior, the Model's brother is a juvenile delinquent— the Parking Meter Bandit. Model realizes Junior is still a cop and quite valiantly pretends that she's just been stringing Junior along. She calls him a squirt and a jerk, gets on the bus without him, and leaves him in the dust as he runs alongside the bus.

"It sounds very corny as I describe it, but if you read that story right now, it would still be quite powerful. It's one of the most powerful things Gould ever did."

Most comic book publishers believe that young boys are not interested in love stories. Collins has a different point of view. "It's the fault of the writers and artists they're not daring to do real stories. It's the fault of the writers and artists who are underestimating their audience and having contempt for the people who are keeping them in business.

"I *constantly* think audiences are underestimated. There *are* dummies in the audiences, and audiences *can* be mobs, but most readers have got something on the ball. If someone picks up a paperback mystery or a science-fiction novel or a comic book, it indicates intelligence. This person has been attracted to the written word. Even if it is the written word floating in balloons and captions above colorful pictures, it *still* reflects intelligence and imagination. Otherwise he'd be home sitting in front of the TV, doing something more passive."

"When I was reading (the Harvey DICK TRACY comics)," Collins continues, "I was hitting a really good period. The stories ended on a terrific cliffhanger. In one ending of a *'Model'* story chapter, for instance, Model is accidentally shot by her juvenile delinquent brother. You see the bullet go through her, then you have to wait a month. That's what got me. I had to wait a month to see if she was going to live. She died, which got me again.

"I didn't expect her to die even though I waited that whole month. That had an emotional impact on me. It told me some very basic things about storytelling, and some very basic things about suspense. It was a good example of violence being used in a story in a positive way."

In one of the DICK TRACY stories Collins wrote, Sparkle Plenty is shot and one character makes reference to Model. Collins says, "Junior made reference to the Model shooting. It was one of my ways of paying tribute to

Chester Gould and Max Collins at Gould's Woodstock, Illinois home in 1981.

Gould, by including a panel of Model and Junior together. Junior talks about his fate, to have the women he loves struck down by violence. Of course, I struck his wife down with violence when I blew her up in that car.

"One sad thing is that Chet doesn't really remember the Model story. It was just a throwaway to him. If I point it out to him, I'm sure he'll remember it, but I know that it was not a story that meant anything special to him. He doesn't think it was one of his best stories."

Many Tracy fans love the stories of the 1930s best. Others prefer the science fiction elements introduced during the 1960s. Collins prefers the stories of the 1950s.

Collins notes that it is uncommon for a fan of a strip such as himself to take over writing it. "It's common in comic books," he explains, "but very unusual

**Hal Schuster,**
based on an interview by Peter Sanderson with the permission of the original publishers

in a major syndicated comic strip. That does not put the onus of 'fan' on me. I was a published professional novelist at the time I was approached, but I came up through reading Chester Gould. Then I read Dashiell Hammett, Raymond Chandler and Mickey Spillane. Gould *led* me into mystery writing. My desire to be a cartoonist led into my desire to be a mystery writer."

Collins explains how he first began writing. "I started writing mystery books in the ninth grade. My parents were very good to me," he says, "they underwrote me to the degree that they didn't make me go out and get a job in the summer. They let me stay home and write a book. I'd spend the school year trying to market it. It would come back from five or six publishers and I realized it was not going to sell. I repeated this process all the way through high school and into college, for a total of six or seven of these unpublished novels. On the seventh one, I came pretty close. I got a very nice letter from the editor at Gold Medal. The editor pointed out that I was doing something that was very common with writers who come out of a fan mentality. I was writing books that came out of books.

"There's a famous story that I've heard, and I don't know if it's apocryphal or not, about Harlan Ellison and Sir Cyril Kornbluth. Ellison at this point was just getting started, and resented the fact that these old-guard people were treating him like a punk. At the same time, he was coming on as a punk, and getting off on it. Ellison did a lot of work that was of first-rate quality, and he deserved more respect than he was getting. What Kornbluth said to him applies to Ellison and to many of us. It certainly applies to my unpublished books. He said, 'You know, Mr. Ellison, a real writer sits down at his typewriter, and he takes his life which he has lived, for good or for ill, exciting or boring, and he turns it

into fiction. His stories are once removed from reality. You, Mr. Ellison, read that man's stories and sit down at your typewriter and make up stories that come out of what you've read, which makes your stories twice removed from reality. And that is why you'll never be any damn good.'

"What's wrong with a lot of genre writing is that it comes out of other genre writing. I was doing that. I was reading Spillane, Chandler, all these people, and my stuff was coming directly out of there. With *BAIT MONEY I* was coming very much out of Richard Stark. (Richard Stark is a pen-name for Donald E. Westlake.) What I also did in that book was draw from my own life. I wrote about my own area. *Every* place in those books is someplace I have been. Any building is a building I have been in. Any room is a room I have been in. The bank that is robbed in that book is the bank where my wife worked; she and I worked out a real robbery. (The character) Jon reflected my interest in comic books and gave me a point-of-view character. So while perhaps 50% of it was coming from Richard Stark, I was taking my life and turning it into fiction."

Besides writing, Collins has also had an interest in other arts. His progression has been an odyssey of sorts. He says, "Let me just describe it like a story. You fall in love with the arts. It might be the movies or it might be *the*-ater; it might be mystery novels or it might be comics. In my case, it was a number of things. I worked as a professional musician for a while. I've done some theater—there have been various areas of the arts I've done professionally. You get into one of those areas because you love it. You want to write books because you love to read books. Then once you learn how to write books, you can no longer read a book as just a reader. You read it as a writer. You read it as a professional.

"It is very difficult thereafter to check your brains at the popcorn counter and go in and sit down and watch the movie. It's very difficult to do that because you *know* the techniques and it's also your competition. You're checking your competition out. So, it has to be pretty good to grab you. I'm not saying that my perspective prevents me from being excited by some books or movies. *RAIDERS OF THE LOST ARK* worked on me pretty darn good. Even though I was watching the technique, it was so good, I was thrilled. It increases your appreciation of the masters, but it decreases your ability to have dumb fun.

"In the mystery area, I reread Spillane, Hammett, Chandler. I continue to read Donald E. Westlake, Ed McBain. There's a few others. James M. Cain is one of my heroes. Jim Thompson.

"I'll tell you a little secret. One of the ways I judge other writers in the mystery area is if they tell me their favorite mystery writer is Chandler, and they think Chandler's better than Hammett. To me, that's a key. This is just my personal bias; it doesn't mean anything, really. I believe Hammett was it.

"Without putting on my college professor hat (I did teach college for six years—I'm not proud of it but I did it), I'll just say Hammett is artistically superior. I find that Chandler uses twelve words and Hammett uses ten. Chandler wrote the same book over and over again—they always had the same characters; the crazy doctor, the gangster. There's a certain pattern there that is exactly the same.

"Chandler is a little bit self-consciously literary, not really a tough guy. I do not really sense a tough man behind that prose. I do not believe Phillip Marlowe as a tough character. I think it's phony.

"Hammett was an ex-Pinkerton operative and the books are usually done in the third person. I shouldn't say that—three of his five novels are actually done in the first person. Even when it's in the first person, he has a much more objective style. In his five novels, he created everything. Every major kind of detective novel there is.

"In *RED HARVEST,* he invented the Mickey Spillane novel of vengeance, the tough guy avenger.

"In *THE DAIN CURSE,* he invented the Chandler kind of novel, the Ross MacDonald type of mystery with the elaborate solution hidden in the closets of a family's past.

"In *THE MALTESE FALCON,* Hammett invented the traditional private-eye novel, and wrote the best one of all time.

"In *THE GLASS KEY,* he wrote the crime novel in which the detective is an amoral non-detective. He actually is the bodyguard of a politician. He did the detective novel where the guy is an amateur detective, but hardly a beginner. He is very much a tough guy. While Hammett didn't invent that—that had been done before—he perfected it and set the standard for that kind of book.

"In the fifth book, *THE THIN MAN,* he did Nick and Nora Charles, the light comedy of manners being brought to the tough mystery story. Yet it was still a tough mystery story.

"I've said some bad things about Chandler, now let me say some good things. While he doesn't ring as true as Hammett, and is a little pretentiously literary, Chandler's Philip Marlowe is a very charming character. The metaphors are terrific. There is a wonderful mood to those books, and they're often very witty. I often have a great deal of fun reading them. He is among my ten favorite writers, maybe in the top five. I think very highly of him, and I only say the negative things about him to try to pull it into perspective.

"I do the opposite game with Spillane. Spillane has flaws, but Spillane is so underrated I dwell on what he did right. I could say the same things about Spillane; I could tell you exactly what's wrong with Spillane, but he is so misread and so under-rated.

"People are starting to look on him as a grand old man of the mystery novel. I'm glad to see that—I'm glad to see him getting some attention—but I find it incredible that it's at this late date. Mickey Spillane invented one of the great detectives of all time, Mike Hammer! There are only three great tough detective writers—*three:* Hammett, Chandler, and Spillane. Everybody else is an imitator. The goal is always to do it better than *THE MALTESE FALCON,* if *anybody* can do that.

"It's a weird situation, where you have a guy coming in and in effect writing the first book in a genre, and doing the *best* one. Why wasn't he content just to invent the genre—why did he have to go and write the best one?

"I don't put (Arthur Conan) Doyle (the creator of Sherlock Holmes) on a literary level with Hammett. I put Hammett on a level with F. Scott Fitzgerald. He is very high on the American literature list."

It is always difficult to define the difference between art and craft. Collins took a stab at it. "I think the Model story (in DICK TRACY) was art," Collins says. "Hammett and Chandler both were art. Where Hammett had it over Chandler was that Chandler was self-consciously *trying* to do art. He should've been doing craft, and because he was a genius, art would've just happened. While I do know Hammett had pretensions toward art, he was basically a writer trying to make a living. He drew upon his life. He drew upon what he knew. It all fit in, and he created art. One of the reasons Hammett stopped writing in the early 1930s, although he lived until the early 1960s, is that he started to get self-conscious. He was afraid he might be creating art and couldn't handle it. He was quoted once as saying, 'When you know that you have a style, it's all over.' He's saying that when you become self-conscious, and you know people are seeing you as an artist, then you're in trouble. You *have* to concentrate on your craft.

"I don't know if you know this about Hammett, but he was tubercular and 50% disabled. He really couldn't hold down regular jobs. He wrote because he *had* to get some money. It was only the fact that he had a pension for his 50% disability, because he'd been in the service, that he was able to struggle along. The funny thing about Hammett is when he started making money, he couldn't write anymore. He lived the majority of his years out on his *THIN MAN* residuals. They were paying him $500 a week for the *THIN MAN* radio show, which he didn't have anything to do with.

"He *despised* the characters. He came to despise them because of the movie series, which he did write, at least the first two. He didn't write the screen plays, but he did write the screen stories, and they were very fully fleshed out. He had to go back and write those characters again, which he disliked doing. He hadn't done a real sequel since the Continental Op stories. He did hack out a couple of *SAM SPADE* short stories in his later career.

"Hammett was once quoted as saying, 'There may be better writers, but there's nobody who's created a more insufferably smug pair of characters than Nick and Nora Charles. I take a perverse pride in that. No one's come up with anything quite as obnoxious as them.' That was a very self-deprecating remark.

One problem in taking over a popular comic strip is that it comes with a long history. DICK TRACY came with fifty years of prior stories. Collins explains, "Well, I have a great deal of respect for what Chet did. I feel very fortunate to have an artist who's worked on the strip for sixteen years; Rick Fletcher was Gould's assistant. That helps give it a nice continuity. I came

into the catbird seat, and sat down. I really lucked into my situation.

"On the other hand, there are certain pressures put upon me, simply because I'm following in the footsteps of Chester Gould. It's like, 'Well, Conan Doyle is retiring now, would you like to write some *SHERLOCK HOLMES* stories?' That's a tough one.

"I approach Tracy as modern-day. I try not to get carried away with the nostalgia, although I obviously have an affection for the history of the strip. I try to be consistent with what Chet did. I try to maintain the traditions of the strip, and I put little touches in that the fans will get a kick out of. I do not let nostalgia become the over-riding aspect of the strip.

"We've gotten a lot of publicity for (our emphasis on contemporary crimes). There was a skyjacking which the media claim was patterned on the skyjacking in my script. It's very important for Tracy to be dealing with modern-day crimes; computer crime and the art heist we patterned upon the very famous art heist. We've done punk rock. There's an inner-city arson case which we did not too long ago. Then there was a corporate kidnapping story which got us a write-up in *TIME*."

Every writer approaches his craft differently. Collins explains how he works, "I am sixteen weeks ahead on the continuity, and I plan the stories about twenty weeks ahead. I have to do a fleshed-out synopsis of the story for two reasons. The syndicate has to see it to approve it. With the exception of once, they've always given me the complete go-ahead.

"The other reason is that the artist needs to have the synopsis ahead of time so he can start working on the villain, because the visual look of the villain in the *DICK TRACY* strip is the key to the character. We pass drawings back and forth—I even do rough drawings sometimes. It often goes through a two or three-stage metamorphosis so we need four or five weeks before the actual story begins.

"I had conceived the 'Ownley Chylde' story prior to the Mark David Chapman incident, and I saw echoes there, precognition or whatever you want to call it. I considered yanking the story, then I thought. 'It's obviously not going to be the same as Chapman.' The similarity is that he was a guy who apparently idolized Lennon, and idolized the Beatles. He was a Beatles fan, as many of us were. A very good friend of mine who had some mental problems could have been Chapman. He was in rock and roll bands with me and wanted to be Lennon. He identified with him that much. It occurred to me that Chapman was a Lennon collector. He collected everything that had to do with John Lennon. Finally there was only one thing left to do, collect Lennon. He collected his life.

"What I did with Ownley Chylde—and again, I had the basic story prior to Chapman—was say, 'Okay, we'll have a Sparkle Plenty collector.' He's got the dolls, and he's got the games and he's got the toys. He's got the comic books. What is there left for him to collect but Sparkle Plenty? Now, he is not going to kill Sparkle Plenty. He wants to marry her, but he doesn't care if she wants to marry him. As a collector myself, I am aware that at the root of collecting is an unhealthy nature we all have."

Fictional characters have traditionally been timeless, yet DICK TRACY is strongly rooted in reality. Collins explains how he handles the aging of his characters. "Tracy had a birthday party, and they brought him a cake with candles and the whole works, and he becomes fifty years old. He will probably remain fifty years old. I think that's old enough, and we'll keep him ageless. Tracy ages—now that he's fifty, he'll stop aging, but until now I considered him aging one year for our two. When the strip started he was twenty or twenty-five, and fifty literal years have passed since. For him only twenty-five years have passed. That's my justification in my mind.

"In the early days of Sparkle's involvement with the strip, Sparkle was very popular. Remember the Sparkle Plenty dolls (prior to Snoopy and Charles Schulz the Sparkle Plenty doll was the number-one comic strip related toy in history). For the first five or even ten years of her life, Gould actually celebrated Sparkle Plenty's birthday in the strip. He would slow the action down and say, 'Excuse me folks, we're going to interrupt the action today, because it's Sparkle Plenty's birthday.' She would be eight years old, and there would be a cake, and there would be Gravel Gertie, and there would be B.O. Plenty. Because he had done that a number of times, when I put Sparkle in this life-or-death situation, and it was coming close to her actual birthday, I thought, 'Why not do the birthday?' It was a nostalgic footnote. We could go back to 1947 and have a picture showing her as the longhaired baby being slapped by the doctor. It was a sweet idea."

Collins says he humanizes DICK TRACY "by bringing family in and showing human frailties. It seemed to me that in the last ten years Chet did, Tracy had become a kind of a symbol of law and order even to him; a symbol of right and wrong, of America. He was an icon. Part of that is built into the design of the character. After all, this guy's face is like a ship's prow. Metaphorically, that's nice, because that razor-sharp profile cuts right through the essence and gets to the solution in time. I think the symbolism is natural.

"Gould had put the family life of the detective in the background, and the symbolism had come to the forefront. Gould stressed the law and order side, and I'm not talking just of police science here. I'm talking about almost a political law-and-order aspect. That was in the 1960s and early 1970s when cops were being called pigs and the anti-war movement was happening. Gould wanted to come out fully and squarely behind the police.

"To me, that was dangerous for a couple of reasons. One, you're getting into a political area and you don't really want Tracy identified with the police in that political sense. The other aspect was that Tracy became less of a character. The more of a symbol he is, the less of a character he is. That was the reason I brought things in like the family life, the child. In the first story, I had him kidnapped and stuck down the old deathtrap that Flattop had been trapped in years before. I brought in a revenge story to get some emotion into it.

"Tracy, Tess and Junior have real feeling for each other. It's this huge extended family. I brought in a few others. I brought in a character called Johnny Adonis, who is a young undercover cop who was originally on the art heist case.

"One of the problems with the size of the extended family is that I like all the characters, but there's only so much room for them. I've come up with a major crime squad composed of Tracy and Sam and Lizz and Lee Ebony and Adonis. With the limited space that we have, if I want to show a briefing with all five characters in one panel, it's very cramped. So it's very rare that everybody is there at the same time."

Sometimes Collins mixes the real world into the strip for a bit of a laugh. One such case was when Tracy boarded a plane and the stewardess promptly informed him that she had been reading his stories since she was a kid. Collins elaborates, "He said to her, 'Why aren't you more thorough—don't you know that I could be a skyjacker?' She says, 'Don't be ridiculous, I've known about you since I was a kid—you're Dick Tracy!' And he expresses chagrin not only because that made him feel grandfatherly, but his effectiveness as a detective is slightly hampered by the fact that everybody recognizes him. It was almost a reference to that classic Gahan Wilson cartoon, of Dick Tracy being beaten up by the thugs, because he's tried to go undercover. The idea that Tracy could go undercover with that face is just a little too ridiculous."

During the first several years Collins wrote DICK TRACY, he consulted often with creator Chester Gould. Collins says, "I talk to him once or twice a month on the phone; we're friends, and he's a very gracious man, and is very helpful to me. He likes to consider himself completely retired. If a reporter will ask him, he'll say he has nothing to do with the strip. In point of fact, he is still a consultant on the strip. He is not active in developing plots and he has no veto power over what I do. It's not unusual for me to get a phone call from him, maybe complaining about something, and suggesting that I do it another way. Or he'll call me up liking something. Both of these things happen. If I haven't heard from him, I make *sure* we touch base at least once a month."

DICK TRACY has always been known for featuring police procedural work. Gould felt that Collins had not included enough of this aspect in the strip. As Collins explains, "We talked about his feeling that I didn't have enough law and order and police science in the strip. It is true that I do not emphasize that as much as he did. He had a point, and because of that I worked some crime prevention material in.

"I contacted the Department of Justice, who put me in touch with the 'Take a Bite Out of Crime' program. A bunch of the 'Take a Bite out of Crime' material is going to appear in various strips."

Collins also occasionally sees Gould in person. "My friend Matt Masterson, the foremost DICK TRACY expert in the country, lives in Boston. He and I used to visit Gould quite regularly. We still do every once in a while.

"When we first visited Gould, Gould was drawing this character called 'Bulky.' I had long hair and a mustache at the time and so did Bulky. This was the second time we had seen Gould, and Matt accused him of having drawn me into the strip. He just laughed. He never denied it or affirmed it. Later, Matt wrote an article on all of the villains for an extended Rogue's Gallery that appeared in the Museum of Cartoon Art's catalogue for their Gould show. Of course he said, 'Bulky was patterned on Max Allan Collins.' I think he said Leydon Egg was patterned on himself, since Leydon Egg was bald. Matt is a little short in the hair department and we never have gotten Gould to affirm or deny either one of those.

"I think Matt figured if he put into print, it would become true. It's followed me wherever I've gone."

Incredible villains have always been the hallmark of DICK TRACY, often as popular as the hero himself. Collins explains how he approaches creating a villain, "What I try to do is begin with a subject matter, as opposed to beginning with a villain. I begin with a subject matter and then metaphorically let the villain reflect the subject matter. Plus I make sure the villain's name reflects the villain's personality and perhaps his personal appearance.

"Breakdown is an example of a kind of villain where the name is somehow metaphorically reflective of the character's appearance. He is this big, tough, strong guy who, when he gets in a stress situation, breaks down. In one panel, his suit is immaculate, with its stripes, and his hair has been combed back. He begins to shake and tremble, and says, 'I can't cope, I can't cope,' and the stripes in the suit become jagged lines. His hair is suddenly a mess. Then one of his boys behind him pats him on the back and says, 'It'll be okay, boss.' Through comic strip magic, he is perfectly immaculate again. His hair is back, his suit is pressed again and he's saying, 'Shut up!' As he's combing his hair back in place, the guys are ducking, as if he's going to hit them. Both his appearance and his personality are tied into one nice little package.

"Torcher came about when I had the idea for the arson story. That terrific pun occurred to me. I had done a bunch of cute villains. Art Dekko and Sue Reel were probably the most popular continuity we've done. Several were basically tongue-in-cheek and comical. I thought it time to do an old-fashioned Gould villain, who is really vile, not funny. I wanted to kill one as Gould used to do with his villains. I thought it was time to do something traditional and I wanted him to die by fire. He died in a fiery car crash. I do not show a charred body or a burnt body on a morgue slab with a tag tied to its toe as Chet would have done. I would have liked to have done it, but knowing what the restrictions are today, I handled it off-stage. I thought it was still pretty

effective.

"Torcher's red hair was like a sea of flames, and at the same time suggested the devil's horns. He looked like a cross between Satan and a dragon. He's my favorite villain that Fletcher designed. I sent him photographs of the actor Robert Lansing, and Dan Duryea, a couple other things, and gave him the idea. The design of that character was all Rick's, though."

Besides creating new villains, Collins also brings back the classic foes of past adventures. "My plan was to do one Gould villain a year," Collins says, "and have the rest of them be original. I get to do three to four stories a year. I did Angeltop first, and although that was my creation, oftentimes people tend to write that off because she was Flattop's daughter. I take full credit for that. That was a new villain as far as I'm concerned. So I didn't really count that as a Gould villain; that's Collins and Fletcher.

"Then I followed up with Haf-and-Haf, who was a Gould villain. I did that right away to indicate to people that I could handle a Gould villain.

"Then I did a long two-part story that had to do with Big Boy, the very first villain. I was, in effect, ending the first DICK TRACY story. In that story, several new villains were introduced. Big Boy was not really the villain, he was the envelope around the story. In fact one of our strongest villains, the Iceman, was one of the two villains.

"That was one of the few times I ever got criticism from Gould. He was saying, 'You're doing the old villains too much.' He didn't bring villains back very often, and he didn't approve of my doing that. He wanted me to do my own stuff.

"So I got that from Gould, and I got a surprising amount of mail from fans who surprisingly didn't approve of my doing the old villains. That surprised me. They always were supportive letters, but saying, 'What's wrong with you—can't you do your own villains?' That was like throwing the gauntlet down.

"Since then, with the exception of Mumbles, I've tried to concentrate primarily on my own villains. Even with Mumbles, I brought in secondary villains who were original creations. So, while I've used a certain number of Gould villains, and I also have a great deal of respect for Gould's work, I have taken his advice. Since I only get to do three or four stories a year, I have been inventing my villains for the most part.

"I enjoy creating my own. It's more fun. It's a challenge to see if you can play that game, can satisfy the people who've been spoiled by the likes of Flattop and the Brow, Shaky, B-B Eyes, Pruneface, the Mole and Mumbles. The Gallery is incredible. The imagination of that man was incredible. To be able to satisfactorily fill those shoes is very satisfying."

Gould received both praise and condemnation for bringing science fiction elements into the DICK TRACY strip during the 1960s. Immediately upon assuming the helm of DICK TRACY, Collins did away with the Moon Maid. Collins feels science fiction elements do have a place in the strip, however. He wants to continue "the gadgetry that's appropriate such as the two-way wrist TV. With the cloning story, the cloning turned out to be a hoax. I left a very strong feeling that if this man, Dr. Zy Ghote, were funded to pursue his research, he probably would come up with cloning. The (scientific) breakthroughs that have been made in the strip have not been made in reality yet. I'm willing to take the extra one step, and one step is enough. It was enough for Neil Armstrong— it's enough for me. "When I tried out for the strip, I submitted a synopsis which was the first story, the Angeltop story. I also sat down and reread the last six years of Sunday pages, which I had in my col-

lection. I wrote a ten-page critique of the direction of the strip in the previous six years. I really looked at what had been going on in the strip so that I could say what I thought was right and what I thought was wrong; what I could continue and what I would discontinue. (I said) what characters were going to go and what characters were going to come back.

"Just as Moon Maid and Vera Alldid exited, I brought back the 1950 character—actually, he goes back to 1944—Vitamin Flintheart. He had not been in the strip since 1950. He's a great, great character, and I have a lot of fun with him. I also brought back Jim Trailer, who was an FBI man who had been in the strip in the 1930s, and hadn't been in the strip since the early war years. I did that because Tracy needed an FBI liaison, and I thought, 'Why not use Jim Trailer?' "

Collins concludes by saying, "I think I brought a certain humanity to the strip. I'm also bringing a Gould approach to the strip. I'm not bringing the approach Gould brought to it in the last ten years; I'm bringing the approach he brought to it in the 1950s. That's what I like to think I'm doing. This isn't to say that the approach he used in the 1960s or 1970s was a bad one. It's just that I knew what period of the strip appealed to me most, which is the 1950s. That was the approach that I felt most comfortable with. Now, the 1950s is not usually considered to be as good as the 1940s, so I'm being quirky here. I'm being eccentric about the approach I'm taking."

53

# DICK

# TRACY'S

# RADIO

# PATROL

*Jim Harmon's book THE GREAT RADIO HEROES (Doubleday, 1966) is the first, and still the definitive, book on the subject of the heroes of radio drama.*

The Dick Tracy radio show began with a police car radio booming: "Calling Dick Tracy, Calling Dick Tracy. . . ." Tracy answered, "This is Dick Tracy — ready for action!" and the action began. There were variations, but this is the one from the early Forties I remember best.

Although the program was an afternoon thriller for children, it was at least as well-written as most nighttime TV dramas of today. Many adults listened to such radio shows in the Thirties and Forties, often as a captive audience as their kids tuned in, but often by choice. The better programs, such as THE LONE RANGER and DICK TRACY aimed their fare at adults, hoping the exciting subject matter would drag in the kids. The Tracy series ran from 1935 to 1948, chiefly on NBC Blue, later called ABC.

The show projected an air of mystery during its best period. Dick Tracy offered more than cops firing machine-guns at bank robbers. It was more like THE SHADOW than GANGBUSTERS. Not a slavish imitation of Chester Gould's great cartoon strip with its realistic police procedures and horribly grotesque villains, the radio series did have memorable villains of its own.

One storyline in the late Thirties concerned "The Man with the Yellow Face," a seemingly sinister figure who could appear at will almost any place. Though suspected of dastardly crimes by Tracy, the man may only have been ill with a disease that gave him a jaundiced, yellow appearance. He was not evil, but only wanted to return a sacred Egyptian treasure to its original resting place.

The program of February 8, 1938, fifty-two long years ago, began like this:

ANNOUNCER: When Dick Tracy closed the case involving the Baron and the sub-stratosphere plans, he paid a visit to Scotland Yard and here the great detective found a new mystery. Driden Small, the well known Egyptologist was returning to America with certain treasures he had discovered in the ancient tomb of Tutominal. Small had reason to believe someone was trying to kill him. He asked Tracy to protect him on the voyage to America. Sitting in Small's cabin the first night out, Dick and Pat were startled to see a strange face peering in their window. . .

SMALL: Mr. Tracy!

TRACY: What's the matter, Small? What's wrong?

SMALL: Look there at the window — the Man with the Yellow Face!

TRACY: What?

PAT: Dick — look. Great Scott — that awful face at the window!

TRACY: It's gone, now. Come on, Pat — we've got to find out who it is.

PAT: Yes, and why he was staring through that window.

SMALL: Don't leave me alone! Don't leave me alone!

TRACY: We'll be back in a moment.... Through this door, Pat — that will take us out on deck.

# by Jim Harmon

SOUND EFFECTS: DOOR OPENS AND CLOSES, BOAT WHISTLE.

PAT: I don't see anyone.

TRACY: Neither do I. Probably waste time if we tried to find out who it was now. Got too much of a head start, and it's too dark to recognize anyone. Come on, let's get back to the cabin. There's a few questions I want to ask Driden Small.

PAT: Dick. There's something about that tomb-digger-upper I don't like.

TRACY: We're here to protect him, Pat, not make a friend of him.

What I want to know is why he was so secretive. He hasn't told us the whole story by any means.

PAT: What's your theory, Dick? What do you think he's trying to conceal?

TRACY: Well, I'm not sure. I think he may have stolen something from Tutominal's tomb — something that might be considered very sacred — and those who consider it so are trying to get it back. That's only a wild guess.

PAT: Doesn't sound so wild to me.

SOUND EFFECT; DOOR OPENS, CLOSES

TRACY: Well, Mr. Small, we couldn't find a trace of your friend with the yellow face.

SMALL: Mr. Tracy, I must say I'm surprised. You promised me protection, and then you run off and leave me alone. Why, I might have been murdered.

TRACY: Nonsense. We were nearby. Nothing could have happened to you.

SMALL: I wish you wouldn't treat this so lightly. I'm in very serious danger.

TRACY: I don't treat any of my obligations lightly, Mr. Small!

SMALL: I tell you, the people who are after me are very clever. Not only that, but they have at their command all the forces of evil and black magic.

PAT: So now it's black magic?

SMALL: Yes, black magic and worse. A curse has been set on me.

I know it! I feel it!

The detective and his partner try to calm Small. They take him to dinner on the ship and try to gain more information. The Egyptologist tells them he had seen Yellow Face around Cairo before he left, and each time he had seen that face, he found a Scarab to warn him of his doom. When they escort Small back to his cabin and turn on the light, they see a message begin to appear on the cabin wall, seemingly written by an invisible hand. It reads: "Your hour is at hand. Your end is near. The Black Pearl of Osiris must shine again." On the floor lies a Scarab seal, the warning sign of Death.

*During the story of the Man with the Yellow Face, a new element was introduced.*

In the following day's episode, Dick Tracy quickly develops a rational explanation for the phantom message. It had been written in invisible ink on the wall before they entered. The heat from the lamp brought out the writing, making it seem as if it were written by an unseen hand.

The two policemen find Yellow Face has much more tangible means of asserting his will. In an encounter with Pat Patton, he flings the Irishman over the ship's rail, into the dark waters below. The fearless Tracy follows his partner into the sea and helps keep him afloat until rescuers arrive.

Tracy barely has time enough to dry out in the captain's cabin when he discovers Yellow Face in Small's cabin. The Middle-Easterner has stabbed and wounded Small "in self-defense," he claims. He then threatens Pat with a gun, demanding to know the whereabouts of "The Black Pearl of Osiris."

Though Tracy is without a dry, working gun, he attempts to bluff Yellow Face. He draws the man out. Yellow Face is really Homei Botek, High Priest of Osiris. He wants the Black Pearl which is the sacred heart of the statue of Osiris back from Small. Tracy sympathizes but can't let him kill Small or shoot Pat. Although unarmed, he makes a move to capture Homei Botek and is shot for his trouble.

The gunshot wound is slight, and Tracy carries on to find the Egyptian hiding in the sacred mummy case of the Second Son of Tutominal.

Eventually, the Black Pearl is returned to its rightful owners, and Small becomes a hunted man for his crimes against the Egyptian people.

A later sequence involves a mysterious figure in black who appears to help Tracy and his friends escape several traps. Although looking menacing, he seems a friend of law and order much like The Shadow. Since crossovers of characters, particularly those owned by different publishers, were not done in those days, it couldn't be The Shadow. It might as well have been. This man called himself The Unknown. No recordings, scripts or human memories survive to recall who it actually was. He remains only The Unknown.

During the story of the Man with the Yellow Face, before the encounters with The Unknown, a new element was introduced. Tracy gained a new finger ring for secret messages. A copy of this Secret Ring was offered to listeners as one of hundreds of "premium" offers during the so-called Golden Age of Radio. The barrage of premiums had started with Orphan Annie giving away a Shake-Up Mug for Ovaltine mixed beverages. Tom Mix then offered a wooden model of his six shooter. (The sponsor, Ralston, hoped for a thousand replies. They received three million.) Jack Armstrong then gave away a pedometer to measure how far one walked on a hike.

Dick Tracy offered a complicated set of badges, certificates and secret codes. They helped a listener rise in the Tracy Secret Service Patrol by recruiting new members and eating lots and lots of the sponsor's product, Quaker Puffed Wheat and Puffed Rice. The ranks went from Sergeant through Lieutenant to Captain and beyond. The new ring was a variation on the club paraphernalia.

The offer at the end of the episode began with Junior, Tracy's assistant and adopted son, pounding the gavel.

JUNIOR: The Dick Tracy Secret Service Patrol meeting will now come to order, Patrol members. And the first thing I want to say is — if you haven't sent for your Dick Tracy Secret Ring yet, do it right away before they are all gone.

ANNOUNCER: If you could see the way the letters are pouring in for those secret rings, you'd be amazed.

JUNIOR: If you see some other boy or girl wearing a secret ring, and you can't get one, you'll be mighty sorry.

ANNOUNCER: It's really a beautiful ring, too. It's plated with 14 karat gold and the big, handsome signet with Dick Tracy's picture on it is really a secret compartment for carrying secret messages and notes.

JUNIOR: That's where Dick kept the Pearl of Osiris.

ANNOUNCER: Here's all you do — just tear the tops off five boxes of Quaker Puffed Wheat or Quaker Puffed Rice as soon as they are empty, and mail the five box tops to Dick Tracy, Box L, Chicago for the Secret Ring.

The request for five box-tops was unusual. Most offers required only one box-top, sometimes two. Five would have the kids eating cereal until it came out of their ears. There was no request for "a dime to cover the cost of handling and mailing." Other sponsors, such as Ralston and Ovaltine, sometimes sent their merchandise without requesting cash and only asked for one proof of purchase. The reason for the premium offer was usually to test how many kids were really listening. Sometimes, such as with Quaker, it also seemed aimed at moving product off the shelves. Today, that Tracy Secret Ring is worth fifty to seventy-five dollars. Far less than the five hundred dollar Shadow Blue Coal Ring originally offered absolutely free for the asking, no box tops required.

The secret Ring carried the hawk-nosed profile of Tracy from the comic strip by Chester Gould. Beginning in 1931, the newspaper feature made Tracy the most famous detective in the world, perhaps even surpassing his inspiration, Sherlock Holmes. The plainclothesman tracked down some of the vilest, and most hideous, villains ever seen.

Flattop, whose head resembled his name and the deck of a World War Two aircraft carrier, was the one readers voted best (or Worst). There was also the Blank, Yogi Yama, Littleface and many more.

Chester Gould was born in the small Oklahoma town of Pawnee, where he graduated High School in 1919. Undoubtedly, much of his world view was set by living in this community not many years after the closing of the frontier. Even today, many people in such towns believe strongly in law and order, and that the best way to handle a "bad man" is at the point of a gun. (Not an unreasonable point of view.)

The local newspaper publisher in Pawnee remembered that Gould must have based the scruffy but lovable character B.O. Plenty on a

## Gould always kept in touch with his old home town

man who lived down by the railroad tracks. "He was bearded and chewed tobacco," D. Jo Ferguson said, but was not really as unkempt as B.O.

A lesser known character from the early days of the strip was Chief Yellowpony, an American Indian. Clifford Haga, a Pawnee resident and a cousin of Gould's, believes the artist based Yellowpony on Moses Yellowhorse, a local man who became a baseball pitcher in the National League.

Gould always kept in touch with his old home town in his memories, the strip and in everyday life. He sent special Dick Tracy Christmas cards to Clifford Haga, and his wife, Loudella, and probably others in the community until his death in Woodstock, Illinois.

Another cousin, the local druggist, Orville McLaughlin, remembered that Gould was not the ideal student in school. He spent most of his time in class drawing pictures. "Art was his passion," McLaughlin said.

That passion took him far, even to serious artistic recognition of his primitive style. Yet nothing ever removed him completely from his roots, the source of more characters and situations in DICK TRACY than anyone will ever realize.

A vital element to the success of the Tracy radio show was the writer, George Lowther. He was a wonderfully creative talent. Like most people in radio, whether performer or writers or producers, he never achieved the fame of those in such visual media as movies. Perhaps the public is more visually oriented. Perhaps children, more than adults of the time, could visualize a comic strip hero on radio. The imagination of the average person seemed limited. There was little fantasy or science fiction in radio, movies, comic strips, books or magazines. While Dick Tracy has been praised as the first procedural police detective, and had elements of harsh reality, it always hovered near the edge of fantasy. The two-way wrist radio (later a TV, and later a computer) was fantasy, and not the first or last such element in the comic strip.

The radio series did not copy such devices from the strip directly, but Lowther often wrote it as "atmospheric fantasy." The story often seemed to involve a ghost or person with a supernatural power. Even though the fantasy element was finally given a logical, mundane explanation, the overall effect of the story remained fantasy.

Lowther loved to set up an impossible situation, one with no possible rational explanation, and then explain it. His explanations were often ingenious, but stretched credibility. Sometimes his hero, Tracy, would note that you could believe the supernatural explanation if you preferred.

At various times, Lowther also wrote for the SUPERMAN radio series. He was its announcer/narrator before the more famous announcer, Jackson Beck, took over.

He was lured away by a better offer from Ralston's TOM MIX cowboy-detective series. There he continued to write convoluted mysteries and developed his skills of characterization. He portrayed Western immortal Tom Mix and his friends, his Straight Shooters such as Sheriff Mike Shaw, teenage ward, Jane, and all the rest.

Lowther became further involved with Superman by writing the first full-length novel of the Man of Steel, contributing parts to the mythos still in use today. This talented man helped create the images of three great childhood heroes of the Forties, Superman, Tom Mix and Dick Tracy.

In 1983, for the Fiftieth Anniversary of Ralston sponsoring Tom Mix on the air, I was called upon. I wrote several entirely new episodes, as well as a concluding episode to an old serial by Lowther. The original recordings could no longer be found, and the scripts of the late author could not be located. I still remembered how Lowther had ended the story so many years before. Many of his plotlines for DICK TRACY are equally memorable.

Surviving recordings show that one reason for the popularity of DICK TRACY on radio was Lowther's technique of packing in twice as much story content as other serials. There is a basic format for a quarter-hour radio serial episode. It begins with the resolution of the cliffhanger from the previous day. On radio, the cliffhanger was not always a life-threatening situation such as a car going off a bridge as in a movie serial. It might be simply a character getting a letter and turning pale as he read the contents. Two Los Angeles disc jockeys, Lohman and Barkley, created a satire of an old radio soap opera in the Eighties. After the present trouble was ended, a character would receive a phone call or a letter and it was always, "The worst news I have ever heard in my life!" The next episode of a real radio serial would either reveal that news, or have the one who received it saying it would have to remain secret for the time being. Then a new development would arise.

For Dick Tracy, it might be a report from the laboratory with an analysis of a clue. For instance, infra-red light might bring out a laundry mark on a handkerchief found at the scene of a crime. Dick would go to the Chinese laundry where the mark led him, only to be greeted by an Oriental hatchet swinging in an arc towards his head! End of chapter.

Lowther condensed such chapters into half the time and presented two chapters a day for the "price" of one. The serials took as many days to conclude as an average afternoon radio serial, but they seemed to move twice as fast.

During its peak period during the late Thirties, Dick Tracy was portrayed on radio by Ned Weaver, a busy radio actor. Earlier in the day, he portrayed the noble Dr. Anthony Loring, eternal fiance of Ellen Brown. She was always known as "Young Widder Brown" to the old timers in town. In an interview, Weaver said, "I had to get right off YOUNG WIDDER BROWN and rush over to do DICK TRACY." He paused, then continued, "It wasn't like soap operas today. I mean, I had to get right off *the show*." Weaver's voice was deep, soft and mellow, not really the kind of voice one would attribute to the chisel-chinned detective. Producers thought him ideal. For an even longer time, Weaver portrayed radio's prime-time sleuth BULLDOG DRUMMOND. The actor made a number of movie and TV appearances, though not in starring roles.

## At the height of its success, the Tracy afternoon serial became the first radio series to switch to a prime time slot.

He may be seen in a frequently re-run PERRY MASON episode, "The Case of the Hesitant Hostess." There he plays a gum-chewing head of a model agency, really a front for dope smuggling. It was a fall from grace from playing the famous detective, but all a part of the make-believe world of acting. Weaver passed away in the mid-1980s.

At the height of its success, due to talents like actor Weaver and writer Lowther, the Tracy afternoon serial became the first radio series to switch to a prime time slot. It became a half-hour complete story on Saturday evenings in 1939, replacing the afternoon daily show. I missed hearing my favorite every weekday, but I liked the half-hour show. It involved stories such as Tracy having to take a hand-pumped rail car over a bridge that had been threatened with being blown up. It was a dangerous, even foolhardy inspection trip, but no bomber was clever enough to fool Tracy. He spotted the destructive device and saved the day.

The move to an evening slot may have been premature. The average adult did not like the new and untried. The show went off.

Nearly a decade later, a half-hour series was tried again, after Tracy had reappeared as a daily serial. This time the serial stayed on, and the weekly half-hour was merely a special treat.

Later, in the Fifties, SUPERMAN was briefly tried as a night-time half-hour show. More significantly, the famous JACK ARMSTRONG, THE ALL-AMERICAN BOY was aged to appeal to a more adult audience and became ARMSTRONG OF THE S.B.I., an agent for the Scientific Bureau of Investigation. Armstrong did not prove any more successful with the adult audience than had Dick Tracy.

Tootsie Rolls sponsored a return of Dick Tracy to radio in the Forties, following the unsuccessful 1939 night-time show. Tracy returned first as another afternoon series, but then as a complete half-hour show once a week, on Saturday evenings. The afternoon serial continued, and the Saturday half-hour was completely separate from its story line. The thirty minute story was also sponsored by Tootsie Rolls.

This time Dick Tracy was played for laughs. This 1947 series anticipated the Camp atmosphere of the BATMAN TV series of 1966. For the first time, many of the characters from the comic strip were used on radio. The ham actor, Vitamin Flintheart, became a regular on the show. Gravel Gertie was another outlandish character.

Everything was often played so broadly one could hear laughter from the studio audience. Most programs such as DICK TRACY did not even have live audiences. Obviously, it was there to cue the home audience when to laugh.

The new thirty minute version ran little more than a full season while the more serious afternoon serial continued for several more years. The night-time series may have been ahead of its time. Most people in 1947 preferred a show that was clearly either drama or comedy.

When the radio series resumed in the Forties, it was without the scripts of George Lowther. The afternoon serial became a mundane police show. Tracy tracked counterfeiters of phone ration stamps during World War II, and later went after safe-crackers and highway truck robbers. These later shows never earned the ratings of the earlier series.

The comic strip has endured longer than the radio series, or any of the old adventure radio series. Currently written by mystery novelist Max Collins and drawn by a former Gould assistant, Dick Locher, the feature still appears in many newspapers.

Yet the memory of the radio show lingers for those who remember. There will always be a special echo somewhere in a corner of our minds, "Calling Dick Tracy...Calling Dick Tracy...."

Quaker Oats Badges given as premiums in 1938 and 1939. Badges denote the ranks of lieutenant, sergeant and inspector general.

# DICK TRACY IN THE SERIALS

# DICK TRACY
## (1937)

Directed by RAY TAYLOR and ALAN JAMES
Assoc. Producer: J. LAURENCE WICKLAND
Producer: NAT LEVINE
Based on the character created by CHESTER GOULD
Screenplay: BARRY SHIPMAN and WINSTON MILLER
Original Story: MORGAN COX and GEORGE MORGAN
Photography: WILLIAM NOBLES and EDGAR LYONS
Musical Supervision: HARRY GREY
Supervising Editor: MURRAY SELDEEN
Film Editors: EDWARD TODD and BILL WITNEY
Sound Engineer: TERRY KELLUM

## CAST
RALPH BYRD: DICK TRACY
KAY HUGHES: GWEN ANDREWS
SMILEY BURNETTE: MIKE McGURK
LEE VAN ATTA: JUNIOR
? ? ? ? ? ? as THE LAME ONE or THE SPIDER
JOHN PICCORI: MOLOCH
CARLETON YOUNG: GORDON TRACY (after)
FRED HAMILTON: STEVE LOCKWOOD
FRANCIS X. BUSHMAN: CLIVE ANDERSON
JOHN DILSON: BREWSTER
RICHARD BEACH: GORDON TRACY (before)
WEDGEWOOD NOWELL: CLAYTON
THEODORE LORCH: PATERNO
EDWIN STANLEY: ODETTE
HARRISON GREENE: CLOGGERSTEIN
HERBERT WEBER: MARTINO
BUDDY ROOSEVELT: BURKE
GEORGE DeNORMAND: FLYNN
BYRON K. FOULGER: KORVITCH
ROY BARCROFT: HENCHMAN
OSCAR & ELMER: THEMSELVES

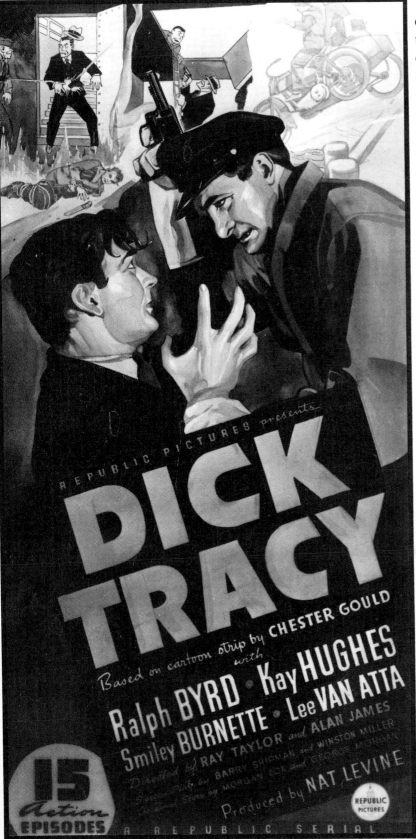

REPUBLIC PICTURES presents

# DICK TRACY

Based on cartoon strip by CHESTER GOULD

with

Ralph BYRD · Kay HUGHES

Smiley BURNETTE · Lee VAN ATTA

and ALAN JAMES

Directed by RAY TAYLOR and ALAN JAMES

Screen Play by BARRY SHIPMAN and WINSTON MILLER

Original Story by MORGAN COX and GEORGE MORGAN

Produced by NAT LEVINE

REPUBLIC PICTURES

15 Action EPISODES

A REPUBLIC SERIAL

In 1936 Republic Pictures purchased their only comic strip property successful enough to spawn a sequel. Not only did it win a second outing in chapterplay form, but a third and fourth as well. The series outdistanced even Universal's popular FLASH GORDON, of which they filmed but three. Republic's series consisted of DICK TRACY (1937), DICK TRACY RETURNS (1938), DICK TRACY'S G-MEN (1939) and DICK TRACY VS. CRIME, INC. (1941).

By the mid-Thirties characters from comic strips and pulps were popular fare for the screen. Universal had already developed several characters, including Flash Gordon and Secret Agent X-9. They passed on Dick Tracy. Columbia also passed. In 1936 their serial division was still being organized. Thus Republic Pictures finally secured Tracy.

The owners of Dick Tracy apparently felt they could have struck a better deal if the other studios had bid.

In the serials Tracy changed from a policeman into a G-Man to broaden the scope of his adventures. The F.B.I. filled the news in the Thirties, capturing notorious gangsters. Republic hoped to tie into the excitement.

Other major changes from the newspaper strip included changing all the supporting characters except Junior (Lee Van Atta), the orphan Tracy takes under his wing. The serial never explains Junior's name, but the comic strip has Tracy adopt the boy who then takes the name "Dick Tracy, Jr." He wants to grow up to fight crime just like Dick Tracy.

This serial also gave Dick Tracy a brother, Gordon. Richard Beach plays the attorney in the character's first appearance. When the Spider Gang captures Gordon, the medical genius Moloch (John Picorri) performs brain surgery. After that, Gordon can no longer distinguish right from wrong and his altered facial muscles distort his appearance. Carleton Young assumes the part of Gordon from that point on. He adds a white streak to his hair, not unlike that seen on Humphrey Bogart in the 1939 RETURN OF DR. X. Tracy searches for his brother throughout the film without realizing he is now part of the Spider Gang.

Carleton Young was an excellent actor and infuses the evil Gordon Tracy with icy menace. Although some incorrectly regard

**By the mid-Thirties characters from comic strips and pulps were popular fare for the screen.**

Young's performance as deadpan, he actually plays Gordon with much subtlety. Even though Gordon speaks in clipped sentences and displays little emotion, there is tension in his face and eyes. This is very difficult for an actor to project. It is evident in the occasional use of a particular closeup which shows Gordon with a menacing stare enhanced by a scar on his right cheek. The scar is a reminder of the car accident in which the Spider Gang captured him.

As Gordon Tracy, Carleton Young projects a definite presence on the screen that draws your eyes to him no matter what scene he's in. When he masquerades as a lawyer summoned by a group of bankers to oversee the sale of a gold mine, he stands out as totally unlike anyone else. You expect someone in the group to leap up and run out rather than remain in the dominating presence.

Carleton Young appeared in other serials such as ZORRO'S FIGHTING LEGION (1939) where he had a small role as Juarez, the ruler of Mexico. He was very good in his appearance as a heavy in SPY SMASHER (1942). Young also appeared in the 1936 anti-drug film about marijuana, TELL YOUR CHILDREN, re-released in the Seventies under the title REEFER MADNESS.

The excellent Ralph Byrd played Dick Tracy. Besides his four Dick Tracy serials, Byrd also starred in BLAKE OF SCOTLAND YARD for Victory Pictures, S.O.S. COAST GUARD opposite Bela Lugosi, and, in 1947, in THE VIGILANTE (from DC comics) for Columbia. Without Byrd, Dick Tracy would not have been as effective on film.

Byrd also portrayed Tracy in two feature films in 1947, DICK TRACY'S DILEMMA and DICK TRACY MEETS GRUESOME, as well as in a short-lived 1952 television series.

This 15 chapter serial released in 1937 is the only one of the four Dick Tracy serials never to be re-released. It was directed by Ray Taylor and Alan James.

Ray Taylor was co-director of the serials THE VIGILANTES ARE COMING (1936) ROBINSON CRUSOE OF CLIPPER ISLAND (1936), FLAMING FRONTIERS (1938, again with Alan James) and THE SPIDER'S WEB (1938). He was sole director of THE JADE BOX (1930), FINGERPRINTS (1930), DANGER ISLAND (1931), BATTLING WITH BUFFALO BILL (1931), THE AIR MAIL MYSTERY (1932), HEROES OF THE WEST (1932), JUNGLE MYSTERY (1932), CLANCY OF THE MOUNTED (1933), PHANTOM OF THE AIR (1933), GORDON OF GHOST CITY (1933), THE PERILS OF PAULINE (1933), PIRATE TREASURE (1934), THE RETURN OF CHANDU (1934), THE ROARING WEST (1935), TAILSPIN TOMMY IN THE GREAT AIR MYSTERY (1935), THE PHANTOM RIDER (1936) and others.

The villain of the serial is a deformed figure referred to in the title cards as The Lame One. In the serial he's called The Spider by Tracy. The Spider moniker may have been deliberately downplayed because of the hero pulp of the same name. THE SPIDER was a widely read magazine in 1936. The disguise used by the hero of the pulp was similar to the guise adopted by "The Lame One" in DICK TRA-

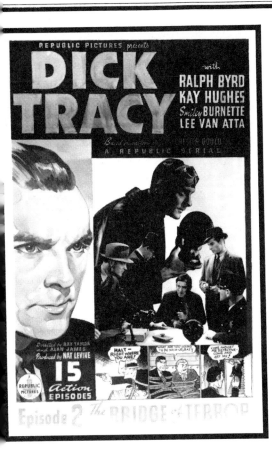

CY. In fact, the Tracy villain looked more like the pulp character than the licensed version presented by Columbia Pictures in their 1938 serial THE SPIDER'S WEB. Adding to the confusion, the Spider Gang shined a spider light on the forehead of their victims before they shot, then branded them with a spider symbol. In the pulp, The Spider branded those he killed with a spider symbol on their foreheads.

The Lame One wore an oversized shoe and dragged one foot as though hobbled. It was actually an elaborate disguise but no hints appeared until his unmasking in chapter fifteen. We suspect something only because his face is never clearly shown but always obscured by shadows.

The monstrous aspect of the Lame One begins in chapter one when a crony rebels and flees his vengeance. We see the man running down a darkened street while the slow, scraping shuffle of the Lame One follows. How a running man fails to escape the slow-moving Spider is not clear. The man finally falls victim to the sign of the Spider.

John Picorri—misspelled on-screen as "Piccori"—plays The Lame One's assistant, Moloch, a hunchback. We often see him carrying around a cat. At one point he expresses interest in an experiment to put the cat's brain into the G-Man's body.

John Picorri appeared in a very similar role in FIGHTING DEVIL DOGS (1938) as the assistant to that serial's villain, The Lightning. That serial contains stock footage from DICK TRACY, particularly sequences involving the Flying Wing. In FIGHTING DEVIL DOGS, Picorri appears almost only in The Wing. His role in DICK TRACY is much larger.

One small role in DICK TRACY featured an actor making his film debut. This actor would go on to become a well known supporting player, particularly in Republic films. The extra, lurking in the background of the control room of the Wing is Roy Barcroft. He became a popular heavy in B-Westerns and played the chief villain in the serials MANHUNT OF MYSTERY ISLAND (1945), THE PURPLE MONSTER STRIKES (1945), G-MEN NEVER FORGET (1947), FEDERAL AGENTS VS. UNDERWORLD, INC. (1948), GHOST OF ZORRO (1949), THE JAMES BROTHERS OF MISSOURI (1949), DESPERADOES OF THE WEST (1950), DON DAREDEVIL RIDES AGAIN (1951), RADAR MEN FROM THE MOON (1952) and others. In the Fifties he played both protagonists and antagonists on various TV shows such as THE LONE RANGER.

As in many Republic Serials, one prime ingredient of DICK TRACY was special effects. Howard Lydecker provided spectacular effects, including the famous Flying Wing model. While stock footage reappeared in FIGHTING DEVIL DOGS, some of the best scenes of the awesome aircraft remain solely in DICK TRACY.

There are beautiful shots of the Wing in flight through clouds. The most impressive scene appears in chapter one when the Wing flies over the massive Oakland Bay Bridge. Republic was allowed to film on the bridge prior to the opening in 1936. They shot footage of the empty bridge from various angles and used them as views of the bridge seen through the canopy of the huge aircraft. There are also excellent shots of the control room of the Wing viewed through the windows of the Bay Bridge below as the craft flies over.

During this sequence, in stark contrast, the overhead shots of traffic clustered on the bridge are obvious model shots when seen on a theater screen. People today only view the home video where the model shots look okay, but the spectacle of the Wing is lost.

The first Dick Tracy serial did not feature spectacular fights. Unlike later Republic serials, fights are no better staged than those of Universal and Columbia. Men hurl themselves at each other and flail away until somebody falls. Stuntmen such as Dave Sharpe (who appeared in a small role in DICK TRACY RETURNS) and Yakima Canutt could have delivered elaborate, carefully choreographed stunts. All the DICK TRACY serials relied on a good plot rather than frequent fights. DICK TRACY relied on a fast-paced story, occasional fights, chases and a few nice stunts. Only later were fights and stunts combined in the Republic serials.

## The first Dick Tracy serial did not feature spectacular fights.

Another new character in the serial was Mike McGurk, played by Lester "Smiley" Burnette. He provided comedy relief in the role of the bumbling assistant. Smiley Burnette later became well known as Gene Autry's sidekick, Frog Millhouse. The name attached to him because of his ability to talk in a strange, bass voice which sounded like a bullfrog croak. He lapsed into this voice on occasion in DICK TRACY.

When he was supposed to be nervous, his voice rose and fell in pitch. In one scene when he's supposed to be reading a speech over the radio, he seems completely oblivious that he's making a fool of himself.

Mike McGurk hung around Junior. While his role could have been overdone, McGurk acted like an F.B.I. agent. He held crooks at gunpoint when the occasion demanded it.

Burnette had appeared in three other serials prior to DICK TRACY. Those were THE ADVENTURES OF REX AND RINTY, THE MIRACLE RIDER and UNDERSEA KINGDOM, all in 1935. In the Forties Burnette made Westerns with Sunset Carson and Charles Starrett. At the time of his death, Burnette was appearing on television in the recurring role of a train engineer on PETTICOAT JUNCTION.

# DICK TRACY RETURNS
## (1938)

Directed by WILLIAM WITNEY & JOHN ENGLISH
Assoc. Producer: ROBERT BECHE
Based on the character created by CHESTER GOULD
Screenplay: BARRY SHIPMAN, FRANKLYN ADREON, RONALD DAVIDSON, REX TAYLOR, SOL SHOR
Photography: WILLIAM NOBLES
Musical Score: ALBERTO COLOMBO
Production Manager: AL WILSON
Unit Manager: MACK D'AGOSTINO
Film Editors: HELENE TURNER and EDWARD TODD

## CAST

RALPH BYRD: DICK TRACY
LYNN ROBERTS: GWEN ANDREWS
CHARLES MIDDLETON: PA STARK
JERRY TUCKER: JUNIOR
DAVID SHARPE: RON MERTON
MICHAEL KENT: STEVE LOCKWOOD
LEE FORD: MIKE McGURK
RAPHAEL BENNET: TRIGGER
JOHN MERTON: CHAMP
JACK ROBERTS: DUDE
NED GLASS: THE KID
EDWARD FOSTER: JOE HANNER
ALAN GREGG: SNUB
REED HOWES: RANCE
ROBERT TERRY: REYNOLDS
TOM SEIDEL: HUNT
JACK INGRAM: SLASHER
GORDON HART: CARSON

When the 1937 Dick Tracy serial proved to be a hit for Republic Pictures, they immediately instituted plans to produce a sequel. Originally announced as THE RETURN OF DICK TRACY, many boardroom discussions went on regarding it. A clause in their original option for Dick Tracy granted the studio rights to use the character "as part of a series or serial." Hoping to clarify the wording, Republic consulted two different attorneys. Each delivered an opposite interpretation of the clause. One said Republic had the right to produce a sequel without paying Chester Gould and the Famous Artists Syndicate any additional fees up front. The other attorney convinced Herbert Yates, the president of Republic's parent firm, Consolidated Film Industries, that the studio could be found to have infringed on the Dick Tracy copyright. They could be forced to turn over all monies the sequel brought in. Yates finally decided to exercise their right early to renew their option, coming due October 31, 1937. He secured a two day extension to process paper work. On November 2, 1937, Republic paid $15,000 to exercise their second option and produce DICK TRACY RETURNS.

Republic considered this serial a major production in their 1938-39 program and assigned George Yates and John Rathmell to work on a script. Yates stopped work completing a script for THE LONE RANGER and began the screenplay for DICK TRACY RETURNS. Two months later they delivered their script. As it turned out, the very imaginative screenplay was never used.

The 1937 Dick Tracy serial included science fiction overtones in the form of a flying Wing and the disintegration ray projected from the Wing to destroy the Oakland Bay bridge. The first draft screenplay for DICK TRACY RETURNS also included a device called the "Daycroft Eye." Powered by radium, the secret government device invented by one Prof. Daycroft could zero in both visually and audibly on any source. The device included a viewing screen called a "penetron plate." A super-criminal called The Brain kidnaps Daycroft and his device, and Tracy enters the scene.

Tracy is joined by his assistant Chuck McKee and Audrey Daycroft, the daughter of the kidnapped scientist. The Brain didn't appear in the comic strip until Chester Gould introduced a villain of that name 37 years later in 1974. The unused screenplay described the Brain as covered to his ears in a dressing gown and scarf and possessing only three fingers on his left hand.

In that script version, the Daycroft Eye is a prototype capable only of a limited range of 25 miles. The Brain plots to raise the money to build a larger model by robbing banks. In order to sidetrack his nemesis, Dick Tracy, the Brain creates a pair of gloves etched with Tracy's fingerprints. He leaves those prints at the scene of his crimes, framing Tracy. Tracy obtains a leave of absence from the F.B.I. so he can clear his name. Even without the F.B.I. and its vast

## Headlines of the F.B.I. round-up of notorious gangsters convinced Republic to change Tracy from a police detective to a G-Man.

resources, Tracy is hot on the trail of the master criminal. During his quest, Tracy faces incredible obstacles. At one point he climbs a column of lead, unaware his foes plan to use chained lightning to transform the lead into radium. The Brain disguises himself as a series of three-fingered characters until, in a unique twist, he is revealed as Daycroft. The scientist had gone insane because the government wanted to use his invention without paying him the millions he felt it worth. In this script, Daycroft dies in the climax in a sanitarium fire.

Republic decided the plot bore too many similarities to the first serial, and commissioned another. They didn't want a super-criminal whose identity was unknown although they would return to this familiar approach for the fourth Dick Tracy outing, DICK TRACY VS. CRIME, INC. in 1941.

Headlines of the F.B.I. round-up of notorious gangsters had convinced Republic to change Tracy from a police detective to a G-Man. In 1934 the F.B.I. smashed Ma Barker and her four sons, so DICK TRACY RETURNS pits the G-Man against Pa Stark and his five outlaw sons. The murderous sons of Pa Stark are Champ, Trigger, Dude, Kid and Slasher. Played with relish by Charles Middleton, the vicious Pa Stark becomes more and more hellbent on revenge against Dick Tracy as his sons are killed. Only one of Stark's sons, Kid Stark, is ever captured and brought to justice. Kid Stark is electrocuted off stage, apparently between chapters, as Pa Stark vows vengeance against Tracy. We're never told when the electrocution takes place. The Starks not trying to free Kid Stark from prison indicates that the sibling paid the ultimate price for his crimes.

Pa Stark hates Dick Tracy for opposing him and blames him every time one of his sons dies. He never considers that he brought it on himself when he insisted Kid Stark kill a G-Man laid up in the hospital so that he can't identify them.

Tracy still discovers who's behind the crime wave. Then it's just a matter of tracking the criminals down. Attrition kills most of them and only Pa Stark and Champ live until the final confrontation in chapter fifteen.

Charles Middleton had been appearing as serial villains since THE MIRACLE RIDER in 1935. He cast a long shadow in the serials FLASH GORDON (1936), FLASH GORDON'S TRIP TO MARS (1938), FLAMING FRONTIERS (1938), DAREDEVILS OF THE RED CIRCLE (1939), FLASH GORDON CONQUERS THE UNIVERSE (1940), PERILS OF NYOKA (1942), THE DESERT HAWK (1944), BLACK ARROW (1944), WHO'S GUILTY? (1945) and JACK ARMSTRONG (1947). Middleton appeared in the features MYSTERY RANCH (1932), MRS. WIGGS OF THE CABBAGE PATCH (1934), KENTUCKY (1939), THE GRAPES OF WRATH (1940, OUR VINES HAVE TENDER GRAPES (1945) and many B-Westerns. Born in 1874, the actor died in 1949. His role as Pa Stark was one of his best. His portrayals of Ming the Merciless in the Flash Gordon serials and of convict "39013" in DAREDEVILS OF THE RED CIRCLE are also memorable.

Changes took place even after the script incorporated the menace of the Starks. Chapter nine originally featured Pa Stark kidnapping a bus load of women and children evacuated in the wake of the dam burst in the cliffhanger of chapter eight. It even included Tracy pursuing the bus on a glider! This entire sequence was cut.

After release, the censors cut short bits from chapter one. Most cut scenes showed how crimes were committed. One cut deleted the G-Man played by Dave Sharpe writhing in an iron lung after Pa Stark pulled its plug. The cuts are evident since Republic chose not to redo the soundtrack. They look like splices in the film.

Famous stuntman Dave Sharpe also appeared in many films as an actor. DICK TRACY RETURNS was one of them. His character only appears in chapter one, but it is a pivotal role. When he appears along with Dick Tracy, it seems his character, agent Ron Merton, is being groomed to be Tracy's partner. Then the Starks brutally murder him. This quickly establishes the viciousness of this deadly family.

Dave Sharpe was already one of Hollywood's most accomplished stuntmen. He is regarded as one of the all time best at fights and tumbles. Although relatively short, he doubled for taller actors such as Kane Richmond in SPY SMASHER and Tom Tyler in THE ADVENTURES OF CAPTAIN MARVEL without looking awkward. Leaps and bounds and acrobatic stunts characterize his fight scenes.

Sharpe played one of the main roles in the serial DAREDEVILS OF THE RED CIRCLE (1939). Ironically, in that serial another stuntman doubled for him! Other roles played by Sharpe include appearances in a few B-Westerns and in the 1950 serial THE IN-

VISIBLE MONSTER. Sharpe played a major part in PERILS OF NYOKA (1942) as he very obviously doubled for Clayton Moore in fight scenes. Entire fight scenes, ostensibly involving Moore's character, are quite clearly Sharpe, even on medium shots. Moore's face only appears in close-ups. The action was so swift the director didn't think anyone would notice the substitution. That serial remains a tribute to the skills of the late stuntman.

In CAPTAIN MARVEL (1940), Sharpe stands in for the good Captain for all takeoffs and landings. He really made you believe a man could fly.

The music in this serial was the same as in the first DICK TRACY serial. DICK TRACY'S G-MEN (1939) also used the same music. It wasn't until DICK TRACY VS. CRIME, INC. (1941) that a new musical score was incorporated.

The title card of DICK TRACY RETURNS uses the familiar Dick Tracy Sunday page from December 6, 1936 for the background art.

Many Dick Tracy collectibles appeared in the Thirties, including some spawned by the serials. DICK TRACY inspired a Big Little Book which retold the film story and included many stills. DICK TRACY RETURNS generated a 424 page Better Little Book from Whitman which retold the film story but was illustrated with drawings rather than stills.

One of the most reused pieces of stock footage in Republic serials features a small, speedy Army tank. That footage originated in DICK TRACY RETURNS in chapter three. It reappeared for the first time in DICK TRACY VS. CRIME, INC. and then reappeared in other serials including ZOMBIES OF THE STRATOSPHERE (1952). The hero always commandeers the tank at a train station in order to catch a speeding train stolen by crooks. The hero catches the train then climbs aboard from the tank and engages in a fight with the criminals. Only the close-ups of the hero change. Since Republic heroes tended to shop at the same store, the suits they wore always matched what Dick Tracy wore when he first sped off in the tank in 1938.

Although Ralph Byrd returned in the title role of Dick Tracy, all of the other actors in the film were new, even though the characters portrayed had appeared in DICK TRACY.

## Pa Stark hates Dick Tracy for opposing him and blames him every time one of his sons dies.

791-Ep.8-1

791-E

# DICK TRACY'S G-MEN
## (1939)

Directed by WILLIAM WITNEY & JOHN ENGLISH

Assoc. Producer: ROBERT BECHE

Based on the character created by CHESTER GOULD

Screenplay by BARRY SHIPMAN, FRANKLYN ADREON,

RONALD DAVIDSON, REX TAYLOR, SOL SHOR

Photography by WILLIAM NOBLES

Musical Score by WILLIAM LAVA

## CAST

RALPH BYRD: DICK TRACY

IRVING PICHEL: NICHOLAS ZARNOFF

PHYLLIS ISELEY: GWEN ANDREWS

TED PEARSON: STEVE LOCKWOOD

WALTER MILLER: ROBAL

GEORGE DOUGLAS: SANDOVAL

KENNETH HARLAN: CLIVE ANDERSON

ROBERT CARSON: SCOTT

JULIAN MADISON: FOSTER

TED MAPES: BRUCE

WILLIAM STAHL: MURCHISON

ROBERT WAYNE: WILBUR

JOE McGUINN: TOM

KENNETH TERRELL: ED

HARRY HUMPHREY: WARDEN STOVER

HARRISON GREENE: THE BARON

STANLEY PRICE: DR. SHANG

Due to confusing language in the option agreements, and differing opinions from attorneys, Republic chose to begin production on their third Dick Tracy serial before entering the third option agreement. The option was then renegotiated. Chicago's Famous Artist's Syndicate originally requested $20,000 for a third serial and $25,000 for a fourth. When the dust settled, Republic paid only $12,500 for DICK TRACY'S G-MEN. The studio did agree not to produce any more serials without first exercising their next option and paying an additional fee.

The popular Ralph Byrd returned in the role of Tracy. As with DICK TRACY RETURNS, his name appeared above the title in the film as well as in the normal screen credits. This reassured fans of the previous serials that the Tracy they knew was back again.

Tracy is in charge of the Federal Bureau of Investigation's western division in Los Angeles when the serial opens. Junior and Mike McGurk are not in DICK TRACY'S G-MEN. While Steve Lockwood, Gwen Andrews and his boss Clive Anderson remain, different actors play the roles than in the previous serial.

In an interesting bit of business, the villain, Nicolas Zarnoff, is introduced via supposed newsreel footage documenting the master spy's espionage activities and showing film of his capture by Dick Tracy. The serial opens with the footage, first showing the exterior of the La Reina Theater in Los Angeles whose marquee lists: PARADE OF EVENTS—LATEST EDITION—ZARNOFF CAPTURE. With all subtlety spared, the newsreel refers to Zarnoff as "The most hated man on earth!" This was a very unusual bit of storytelling magic generally not found in the normally straightforward chapterplays. The eleven page sequence was reduced in the serial. Cuts included deleting a real gas chamber and Zarnoff's fate. The well-staged filming prevented it from looking like a real newsreel. Instead it looked like a movie filmed by newsreel cameramen. When Orson Welles' CITIZEN KANE (1940) employed this idea, it was deliberately shot to look like a real newsreel. Rather than showing a movie theatre beforehand, it cut right to the newsreel.

Then the film cut away to a roomful of reporters to establish the setting.

Dick Tracy and his team enter the story, and then, like something out of a Universal horror film, Zarnoff goes to the gas chamber. Later, he revives due to a drug he had ingested in his cell. The drug, supposedly mixed with printer's ink in a newspaper, was an ancient brew developed by the alchemists of Satan. This quickly establishes

him as more than an average Fifth Columnist.

Zarnoff wastes no time resuming his criminal activities. He doesn't care much when Tracy learns who's behind the crime wave.

When Zarnoff revives, a reference is made to his eyes looking strange. It's never mentioned again. Zarnoff is a very exotic villain in chapter one when the style of direction is very moody. The film projects classic film noir.

Tracy's brains and brawn continue to supply the obvious focal point. In chapter one the G-Man suspects a cattleman isn't all he seems. Tracy remarks to the man that, "They tell me that blister rust is cutting down on the herds this year," and we know Tracy isn't making idle conversation. He quickly exposes the cattleman as a fraud and gains a lead to Zarnoff.

Tracy is more of a daredevil than ever in this serial, particularly in a daring escape at the open of chapter two. He escapes an explosives-laden speedboat by grabbing the landing gear of a biplane which swoops down to rescue him. It's not only one of the most impressive stunts in the Tracy serials, it's one of the most impressive in the history of motion picture serials. While Tracy's skill is as important in this rescue as that of the biplane's pilot, at other times Tracy is rescued entirely through the efforts of others. In chapter seven the G-Man is unconscious while a heavy object is being lowered towards him, and only his partner's quick thinking saves him. In chapter nine he's locked in a room filling with lethal gas. When he's rescued by his partner again, Tracy remarks, "Phew, I never did like poison gas!"

At the conclusion of chapter nine historical footage appears when the Pan Pacific Dirigible is set on fire and crashes to the tarmac. Special effects footage intercuts with actual footage of the destruction of the Hindenburg from May 6, 1937. Besides this and the international nature of Zarnoff, there is another reference to the shaky state of world affairs. In chapter 5 a U.S. bank has to re-

linquish reserves because the nation of "Benzobia" wants its gold back due to war fears.

Capitalizing on this, the G-Men try to trap Zarnoff in chapter 12 by announcing that a scientist has developed a "formula to end war." It's a wonder Zarnoff tries to steal it because the film never really explains what the formula is for.

When Zarnoff sends someone to steal the formula, they are supposed to be plucked from the top of a building by an autogyro. This vehicle was a combination airplane and helicopter developed in the Thirties but which never caught on due to the depression. The patents established for the autogyro were crucial in developing a workable helicopter. The autogyro, like the dirigible, is one of those fascinating old flying machines which remain exciting to watch in old films. The January 1990 issue of AIR & SPACE magazine offers an excellent look at the vehicle.

Before the missile, films used the "aerial torpedo." Chapter 14 includes such a device. It looks like a torpedo with wings. Although it is only discussed in this serial, one actually appears in DICK TRACY VS. CRIME, INC.

Before Zarnoff meets his end in chapter 15, his own men almost kill him when he comes up a path to his hide-out. Although they're guarding the hide-out, they're such poor shots they all miss their target! When Zarnoff meets his fate at the conclusion, we only see Tracy and Steve Lockwood standing over the body in the desert. They talk about what happened to him, but the film never shows the actual demise or the corpse. Perhaps they felt it to be bad taste? That notion is odd. We wouldn't actually see a corpse but just an actor lying very still! That was Hollywood in the Thirties!

Irving Pichel played Zarnoff. The actor had previously played Fagin in OLIVER TWIST (1933) and appeared in such films as CLEOPATRA (1934), JESEBEL (1938), JUAREZ (1940) and SANTA FE (1951). Following his role as Zarnoff, he embarked on an even more successful career as a director. He directed over 30 films before his death in 1954. The films include THE MIRACLE OF THE BELLS (1948), MR. PEABODY AND THE MERMAID (1948). For producer George Pal, he directed THE GREAT RUPERT (1950) and DESTINATION MOON (1950). Actually he'd been directing films even before appearing in DICK TRACY'S G-MEN, and worked as the co-director on the 1932 version of THE MOST DANGEROUS GAME. The film is still acknowledged as the most effective version of that oft-told tale.

Phyllis Isley, as Gwen Andrews, was originally billed fourth among the actors in this serial. Phyllis Isley was the real name of the actress who would soon become known by her stage name of Jennifer Jones. She made her motion picture debut in Republic's 1939 Three Mesquiteer Western NEW FRONTIER. The film was later retitled FRONTIER HORIZON when released to television. DICK TRACY'S G-MEN followed close behind under her contract with Republic. The actress was then just 20 years old.

Although she had a five year contract with Republic, her father, P.R. Isley, president of the Southwest Theatres chain, obtained her release. Supposedly the daughter of the theater executive didn't care for film work. The actress soon returned to the screen as Jennifer Jones and won the Best Actress Oscar for 1943 for THE SONG OF BERNADETTE. One of the most haunting performances the actress ever gave was in the 1948 fantasy THE PORTRAIT OF JENNIE. In spite of the sudden rise to fame of their former contract player, Republic did not try to cash in on her notoriety until the 1955 theatrical re-release of DICK TRACY'S G-MEN. Then the advertising art listed Jennifer Jones right after Ralph Byrd with her original billed name of "Phyllis Isley" listed next to it by way of explanation. Unlike other serials where the heroine figured prominently in the proceedings, all of Gwen Andrews' scenes took place in Tracy's office at FBI headquarters in Los Angeles. She delivered all 204 words of her dialogue in 13 of the 15 episodes. This kept faith with the Dick Tracy serials wherein heroines remain in the background rather than being kidnapped or otherwise imperiled.

As in the first and second serials, DICK TRACY'S G-MEN spawned a movie tie-in Better Little Book whose 425 pages retold the story of the chapterplay with drawings instead of stills.

# DICK TRACY VS. CRIME, INC.
## (1941)

Directed by William Witney & John English
Based on the Dick Tracy cartoon feature
created by Chester Gould
Screenplay: Ronald Davidson, Normal Hall, William Lively,
Joseph O'Donnell and Joseph Poland
Associate Producer: W.J. O'Sullivan
Special Effects: Howard Lydecker
Photography: Reggie Lanning
Music: Cy Feuer

## CAST

RALPH BYRD: DICK TRACY
RALPH MORGAN: THE GHOST
MICHAEL OWEN: BILL CARR
JAN WILEY: JUNE CHANDLER
JOHN DAVIDSON: LUCIFER
RALPH MORGAN: J.P. MORGAN
KENNETH HARLAN: LT. COSGROVE
JOHN DILSON: HENRY WELDON
HOWARD HICKMAN: STEPHEN CHANDLER
ROBERT FRAZER: DANIEL BREWSTER
ROBERT FISKE: WALTER CABOT
HOOPER ATCHLEY: ARTHUR TRENT
ANTHONY WARDE: COREY
CHUCK MORRISON: TRASK
C. MONTAGUE SHAW: DR. JONATHAN MARTIN
JOHN MERTON: BRENT
TERRY FROST: DRAKE
FORREST TAYLOR: METZIKOFF'S BUTLER
DAVE SHARPE: VAULT AND BOAT HEAVY

A REPUBLIC SERIAL IN 15 CHAPTERS

# DICK TRACY
## vs.
# PHANTOM EMPIRE

FORMERLY ENTITLED, "DICK TRACY VS. CRIME INC."

with **RALPH BYRD**
RALPH MORGAN · JAN WILEY
JOHN DAVIDSON · · MICHAEL OWEN
Based on Cartoon Strip by CHESTER GOULD
Original screen play by RONALD DAVIDSON · NORMAN S. HALL
WILLIAM LIVELY · JOSEPH O'DONNELL · JOSEPH POLAND
Directed by WILLIAM WITNEY · JOHN ENGLISH

After DICK TRACY'S G-MEN appeared in the fall of 1939, Republic contemplated renewing their option to make another serial. Since this would involve an advance payment of $17,500, they deliberated before contacting Famous Artists Syndicate President Alfred Loewenthal. While expressing interest in renewing the option, they asked that the amount due be disbursed in a dozen equal payments, one falling due each month. Famous Artists accepted and Republic made the first payment on December 22, 1939. This option would last until 1944, which is why the RKO Dick Tracy film series didn't begin until 1945.

Although the previous three serials had not drawn from comic strip plots, DICK TRACY VS. CRIME, INC. found inspiration in a 1940-41 story involving a villain called Krome. The strip offered a villain who wore a full face covering similar to that of an executioner and ran a murder-for-hire business called Crime, Inc. The script writers went one better with a more fantastic villain called The Ghost who wore a full-head rubber mask. The serial villain gained powers of invisibility from the scientific wizardry and criminal cunning of his assistant, known only as Lucifer.

## While the other serials took place in the West, this time Tracy flew to New York City.

The Ghost plotted to found a criminal empire called Crime, Inc. with his late brother, Rackets Reagan. Then Dick Tracy and the Council of Eight brought Reagan to justice and sent him to the electric chair.

Working titles for the serial included DICK TRACY'S REVENGE and DICK TRACY STRIKES AGAIN. Finally the studio settled on the more evocative DICK TRACY VS. CRIME, INC. When Republic re-released the serial later in the Forties, it was retitled DICK TRACY VS. PHANTOM EMPIRE. This name change created confusion since Mascot had released a serial in 1935 called THE PHANTOM EMPIRE. That film made Gene Autry a star.

Some people thought DICK TRACY VS. PHANTOM EMPIRE was a fifth Tracy serial in which he went to the underground empire portrayed in the 1935 serial. The title was a bit of a stretch, as it used the term "phantom" only because of the ability of the Ghost to become invisible.

Exciting new march music played over the opening titles. The main theme appeared nowhere else in the body of the serial nor were there even reworkings of the theme. The title march stood on its own and set a deliberate, exciting tone.

While the other three serials took place in the West, this time Tracy and his new assistant, Bill Carr, flew to New York City. When members of the Council are executed under the very noses of police guards, they call for Tracy. After another victim dies, it takes Tracy fourteen chapters to discover that their nemesis, the Ghost, can make himself invisible.

The Ghost zealously guards his secret, killing those outside his organization who discover it before they can reveal the information. In a dramatic scene, Tracy corners the ghost only to see him disappear. It captures the melodrama of the best action serials.

Although the Ghost was a disguised member of the Council of Eight, he was more daring than other mystery villains. He actually appears in disguise in chapter two, wearing glasses and a goatee to effect the escape of his confederate, Lucifer. Despite his disguised voice, it made it easier for the viewer to guess his identity.

This action is realistic within the context of the story because it's clear the Ghost's strength lies in the invisibility device and its inventor. When the Ghost and Lucifer discover Tracy is jamming the device, the Ghost panics. He stops at nothing to destroy the jamming wave. Tracy doesn't even realize he's jamming the invisibility device!

The Ghost and everything he's wearing turns invisible when the device is activated, yet his gun, once drawn, remains visible. It hangs in mid-air, threatening its intended victim. Why the gun becomes visible while nothing else the Ghost wears or carries shows up is never explained. The reason, of course, is that having the victim talk to empty air is not very interesting. A gun hanging in the air establishes a presence, even if the presence is otherwise unseen.

The story avoids the question of how an invisible man can see. Light passes through him and shouldn't reflect from the corneas of his eyes. There is something vital about the Ghost's mask. When

Lucifer turns invisible to escape from jail in chapter two, he doesn't just put on the medallion, but also the rubber mask!

This is arguably the best of the four Dick Tracy serials. It makes generous use of stock footage from the previous serials in chases and cliffhangers, however. The Army tank and train sequence first used in DICK TRACY RETURNS reappears in chapter three. It serves as a complete sequence rather than as part of a cliffhanger. The cliffhanger from the first chapter of DICK TRACY'S G-MEN appears intact as the cliffhanger in chapter three. It involves an aerial rescue of Dick Tracy from a speedboat laden with explosives. A sequence placing Tracy in a small cabin cruiser crushed between two ships (first used in DICK TRACY) is reused intact in the middle of chapter five. In DICK TRACY'S G-MEN, Tracy is aboard a biplane which tries to warn a train to stop before riding over a bomb on the tracks. Part of this is reused in chapter eight, but a different cliffhanger arises from it. Chapter one presents the most spectacular cliffhanger in the serial as it shows the apparent destruction of New York City. This is stock footage from the film S.O.S. TIDAL WAVE (1939). This footage was reused again as part of the climax of chapter fifteen of KING OF THE ROCKETMEN (1949). Other stock footage includes shots of a missile test and of a group of marines being attacked by criminals. These scenes are from the feature CALLING ALL MARINES (1939). The large use of stock footage does not detract from the serial.

The story is interesting and fast-paced and the script is one of the best in a Republic serial. This serial lacks the slow spots which detract from the other Tracy serials and the episode recapping prior episodes. It possesses a nice atmosphere due to the fantastic presence of the Ghost. Unlike other weird serial villains, he is always at the forefront of the action rather than dispatching others to do his dirty work for him. If someone has to be killed, the Ghost does the deed himself.

Although this is a very visual serial, there was no accompanying Big or Better Little Book for the release.

The miniatures department at Republic received screen credit for the first time. Howard Lydecker, the head of the special effects department, labored anonymously on the earlier serials. This time he received on-screen credit. The miniatures shop appeared in chapter eleven as the setting for a fight in a factory. Miniature wooden oil derricks (constructed for KING OF THE TEXAS RANGERS) even figure in the battle as they're knocked around. Other miniatures appear in the background on tables.

Some good actors appear in this film. John Davidson, who played mysterious characters from both sides of the tracks in other serials, plays Lucifer. Davidson often played foreigners from widely scattered parts of the world. In FIGHTING DEVIL DOGS (1938) he played Lin Wing, an Oriental curio dealer who's killed after revealing The Lightning's plans. In THE ADVENTURES OF CAPTAIN MARVEL (1941) he's the mysterious Tal Chotali. The character seems to be on our side, but acts suspiciously throughout the serial. Even when we know he's a good guy, we can't help feeling he knows a lot more than he'll ever reveal. In PERILS OF NYOKA (1942) he's Lhoba, the Taureg chieftain, but in THE PURPLE MONSTER STRIKES (1945) he's elevated to the position of Emperor of Mars. In CAPTAIN AMERICA (1943) he plays a role similar to that of Lucifer as he's the aid of Lionel Atwill, the deadly Scarab and foe of the title hero. Nearly bald and possessing prominent features, he had looks that enable a character actor to dominate any scene. The only reason we pay more attention to the Ghost when they're together is because of the bizarre hood-mask the character wears. Davidson also appeared in THE PERILS OF PAULINE (1933), BURN 'EM UP BARNES (1934), TAILSPIN TOMMY (1934), and KING OF THE ROYAL MOUNTED (1940).

John Davidson is not a henchman of the Ghost so much as his partner. The Ghost's chief henchman is John Corey, played by Anthony Warde. He played the heavy in a number of serials, his most prominent role being that of the evil ruler of earth in the 25th century, Killer Kane, in BUCK ROGERS (1939). Warde also appeared in KING OF THE MOUNTIES (1942), THE MASKED MARVEL (1943), THE MONSTER AND THE APE (1945), KING OF THE FOREST RANGERS (1946), THE BLACK WIDOW (1947), DANGERS OF THE CANADIAN MOUNTED (1948) and RADAR PATROL VS. SPY KING (1949).

1097-Ep-15-4

# RALPH BYRD

## the man who is dick tracy

*The first actor to portray Dick Tracy on the screen has portrayed the character more than any other. Basil Rathbone as Sherlock Holmes is the only other actor with comparable screen time playing a single role in films.*

Born in 1909, a native of Dayton, Ohio, Ralph Byrd appeared in films prior DICK TRACY in 1937, perhaps his earliest role being in HELL SHIP MORGAN (1931). When he first signed for DICK TRACY in late 1936, he was 27. They paid him $150 a week for his work on the film. In the world outside films, $50 a week was considered very good wages in 1936.

On August 25, 1937, Byrd signed with Republic as a contract player under terms which stated that the actor could only be employed in a film as a star, costar or featured player. The contract stipulated that he be paid an additional $100 per week for any work in a Dick Tracy film during the first year. The first Dick Tracy serial had proven to be a hit for Republic and the popularity of Ralph Byrd in the role was not overlooked.

Byrd then earned $220 a week on S.O.S. COAST GUARD (1937) and $250 a week for both DICK TRACY RETURNS and DICK TRACY'S G-MEN.

On July 9, 1941, Byrd renegotiated his contract and upped his earnings to $1000 a week for his next Dick Tracy serial with a five week guarantee. He was also promised work in at least one feature at $600 a week with a two week guarantee. Under this agreement, the actor would have thirty day's notice to report for work for the next Dick Tracy.

When that notice came, Byrd was already filming the Alexander Korda film JUNGLE BOOK. The start date for DICK TRACY VS. CRIME, INC. conflicted with the final shooting of Korda's film. The screen Actor's Guild mediated and Korda was granted access to Byrd. Republic would be given 48 hours notice, and could deduct for time Byrd was away from shooting. Following completion of DICK TRACY VS. CRIME, INC., Byrd's contract with Republic was not renewed. He never worked for them again.

Prior to signing with Republic in late 1937, Byrd made a serial for Victory Pictures called BLAKE OF SCOTLAND YARD, which, like the Tracy series, was 15 chapters long. His last serial was THE VIGILANTE for Columbia, released in 1947. It too ran 15 chapters in length, although by then individual chapters were shorter in length than what they had been in 1937.

Following the elapse of Republic's last option on Dick Tracy, RKO immediately stepped in and began a series of four feature films. These were DICK TRACY (1945), DICK TRACY VS. CUEBALL (1946), DICK TRACY'S DILEMMA (1947) and DICK TRACY MEETS GRUESOME (1947). The first two films starred Morgan Conway as Tracy. Then the popularity Byrd achieved in the role in four serials convinced RKO to recast him for the last two features.

These were not feature films as we think of them today. They only ran 60 to 65 minutes in length and were intended to run as part of a larger program at a theatre much as serials did. Like the four serials, all four of the features are currently available on prerecorded tape. They appear most often in stores specializing in classic films, although they occasionally turn up at large chain stores such as K-Mart.

Byrd also appeared in DESPERATE CARGO (1941), GUADALCANAL

DIARY (1943), MARK OF THE CLAW (1947) and THE REDHEAD AND THE COWBOY (1951).

An interesting memory of the actor appears in the book IN THE NICK OF TIME (MOTION PICTURE SOUND SERIALS) by William C. Cline (McFarland & Co., 1984). In it the author recalls the time he met Ralph Byrd in the 1940's. In describing Byrd's portrayal of Tracy, Cline writes, "Byrd was a dead-ringer for the Gould characterization. His firm jaw, full, cleft chin, thin-lipped mouth, high cheekbones and piercing eyes, along with a straight, noticeable enough nose, gave the impression that this might have been the face the cartoonist had in mind when he first drew Tracy. In addition to the physical similarity, Byrd also projected the intense dedication to law and order associated with the strip hero. His was an all-business, no-nonsense demeanor that wasted no time on things not directly related to the case at hand.

"This quality became even more apparent when I met and talked with the actor while he was appearing at the Paramount in Concord in the middle Forties. Seeming unusually nervous, Byrd found sitting still quite difficult, was up and pacing when he stayed in a room, darted in and out of his dressing room between shows, and often went to the outer lobby to greet entering patrons — even allowing himself to be ganged up on for questions and autographs on the sidewalk outside. It was as if he could hardly wait to get on with the business of making Ralph Byrd known to every citizen in town. When he did pause for a few minutes for a cup of coffee in the theatre office or to apply make-up just prior to a stage appearance, the talk was of pictures, roles and stories; never of social interests, polit-

ical beliefs or other activities. For a long time afterward, Concord remembered the day Ralph Byrd was in town and often asked us at the theatre when they would be able to see him in a picture again."

Byrd last played Tracy in a half-hour television series for Snader TV Productions that ran in 1951 and 1952. Various sources give contradictory information on the series, variously listing the number of episodes as from 23 to 39. THE COMPLETE DIRECTORY TO PRIME TIME NETWORK TV SHOWS by Tim Brooks and Earle Marsh lists the series as running from September 11, 1950 to February 12, 1951. Besides being only 23 weeks, this is a year earlier than generally believed. But even if it did air a year later, Byrd's untimely death wouldn't have cut the series short as his sudden fatal heart attack struck on August 18, 1952.

Byrd was survived by his wife, actress Virginia Carroll, and a daughter.

**Ralph Byrd, second from left, in BLAKE OF SCOTLAND YARD.**

# DICK TRACY IN THE MOVIES

# DICK TRACY
## (RKO,1945)

*Four years after
DICK TRACY VS.
CRIME, INC., a new
quartet of films
began. They featured
the great detective
restored to his
position in the police
department. Ralph
Byrd didn't play him
this time, at least not
at first.*

Running time: 62 minutes

Music: Roy Webb

Musical Director: G. Bakaleinikoff

Director of Photography: Frank Redman, A.S.C.

Artistic Directors: Albert S. D'Agostino

Ralph Berger

Editor: Ernie Leadlay

Executive Producer: Sid Rogell

Original Screenplay: Eric Taylor

Producer: Herman Schlom

Director: William Berke

## CREDITS

MORGAN CONWAY: DICK TRACY

ANNE JEFFREYS: TESS TRUEHART

MIKE MAZURKI: SPLIFACE

JANE GREER: JUDITH OWENS

LYLE LATELL: PAT PATTON

MICKEY KUHN: JUNIOR

JOSEPH CREHAN: PROF. STARLING

ALSO

TREVOR BARDETTE

MORGAN WALLACE

MILTON PARSONS

WILLIAM HALLIGAN

A man silhouetted under a lampost lights a cigarette, then slips into the shadows as a bus pulls up to the curb across the street. A woman gets out and walks down the darkened street and he follows at a distance. She becomes aware of her pursuer and turns, but finds no one there. She continues walking again down the quiet street then suddenly turns around again. He strikes her down before she can even scream. The man runs off down the street. Another woman comes upon the young woman's body and screams.

A call goes out for Dick Tracy. His dinner plans with Tess Truehart fall through when he has to go down to police headquarters. There the cops grill a kid named Johnny about a payroll robbery. Johnny refuses to talk. Pat Patton tells Tracy about the murder, and the victim's address. "Murder?" Tracy questions loudly. "At 911 Laurel?" This is not the victim's address, but that of Johnny's mother. Tracy uses this ploy to trick the young hood into fingering the real robber. Tracy knew Johnny was innocent but had to get him to talk. He likes to cut corners in the pursuit of justice.

Meanwhile, Tess waits in Dick's office to go out for dinner.

Dick Tracy and Pat go to the murder scene. The victim, a school teacher named Dorothy Stafford, was slashed to death with a sharp knife. Tracy takes her pocketbook back to his office, where Tess is sleeping on the couch. Nothing in the woman's purse indicates she was robbed. The pocketbook contains money. It also contains a note, crudely written and misspelled:

RAP UP FIVE HUNDRED DOLLAR IN SMALL BILLS AND PUT IN ST. SWEEPERS TRASH CAN CORNER OF LAKEVUE AND ASH AT 8 TOMORROW NITE.

It is signed by Splitface.

Tess wakes up, annoyed to find it is almost eleven o'clock. The film fades to a montage of morning newspaper headlines. One reads,

SCHOOL TEACHER KILLED BY MANIAC. WHO IS SPLIT-FACE?

At Tracy's home, his housekeeper takes a call from Pat. Tracy is to meet the Chief of Police at the Mayor's office. Before leaving, Tracy goes upstairs to check on Junior, who is working on a case of his own. Junior fingerprints Tracy and proves that he was the mysterious prowler who raided the icebox late the previous night. The great detective confesses to the crime, but must leave when Pat shows up.

## Tracy makes good on his promise to Tess.

Downtown, the mayor is having a fit. He has received an extortion note signed "Splitface," in the same handwriting as the other note. The note demands ten thousand dollars. The mayor is not reassured by promises of police protection. He wants the mysterious Splitface brought in.

The dead teacher's papers hold references to a Wilber Thomas. None of her teacher friends recognize the name. Pat gets no answer to his phone call, so he and Tracy go to Thomas' house at night. A dog moans in a neighboring yard, and a shadowy figure lurks nearby. Tracy finds another slashed body in the neighbor's driveway. While searching the neighborhood, he sees a figure jump the fence into another yard. Tracy follows and rings the front doorbell.

The owner of the house, Steve Owens, says he has seen no one, but invites Tracy inside to look around. Owens is the owner of the Paradise Club. Tracy offers him a police guard, but Owens declines, surprisingly unruffled by a murder in his own neighborhood.

Other police reach the neighborhood and identify the body as Wilber Thomas, the friend of the slain school teacher. A Paradise Club matchbook lies in the front seat of Thomas' car. Thomas had also received a note from Splitface, demanding one thousand dollars, which he seems to have paid off. The payoff didn't stop him from being killed, however. Tracy is curious. Most extortionists don't vary their demands as much.

Tracy promises to take Tess to dinner that night, but first must join the stakeout of the Mayor's payoff point. The money is placed in the trash can but the extortionist doesn't show. A dog causes a false alarm and the stakeout is called off.

Tracy makes good on his promise to Tess. He insists that he's off duty, but the club he takes her to is Steve Owens' Paradise Club. Owens is out, but his daughter Judith greets Tracy, drawing icy stares from Tess. Judith is evasive about her father's whereabouts and says that she came to the club after being frightened by a man in their garden. Tracy takes the keys to her house and heads there with Tess in tow. Splitface is inside, peering out a window. His face bears a large, disfiguring scar across it.

Tess and Tracy enter the house but the lights are out. Tracy looks for the fuse box, leaving Tess alone in the living room. Splitface sneaks up on her and she screams at his hideous countenance just as the lights come on. Splitface runs from the house.

Tracy and Tess jump into their car and follow the killer's car as it speeds off. A chase ensues through the city streets. Splitface abandons his car, but Tracy is close behind on foot and follows him into an apartment building.

Splitface ducks into a room. When Tracy opens it, he finds a cluttered storeroom with access to the roof. On the roof he finds a man gazing at the sky through a large telescope.

Professor Linwood J. Starling, Astrologist, has been studying the stars since darkness fell and has seen no one. Admittedly, he was preoccupied for, as he tells Tracy, his powers of concentration are great. Tracy insists on searching Starling's apartment. As Tracy sleuths, Starling gazes into a crystal ball and sees two knives. "Two knives dripping blood," he intones, "but there will be twelve more." He prattles on about a cycle that will be completed with fourteen deaths. He seems to be receiving information about a fifteenth death when Pat and the police break in. They interrupt his trance.

Meanwhile, Tracy has found a surgical knife under Starling's mattress. This is enough evidence to arrest the professor despite his protestations of innocence.

Tess doesn't recognize Starling as her assailant, but he seems to have a hypnotic power over her. Tracy speculates that Splitface's scar might be a clever make-up job. Anybody could be Splitface. As they drive off, Splitface watches from a rooftop.

Tess and Tracy return to the Paradise Club, but they are too late for dinner. Judith still doesn't know where her father is. Tracy takes her into protective custody at his house. Tess packs her bags to keep a close eye on things, too.

The knife found in Starling's apartment came from a surgical supply company. They recently sold three such knives to an undertaker. The undertaker, Deathridge, claims all three knives disappeared shortly after their purchase.

At police headquarters, Starling refuses to talk without a lawyer. Tracy plays a simple word association game with him, and the professor balks at the name Deathridge. Tracy and Pat wonder if Starling knows the undertaker.

Tracy asks what comes in groups of fourteen.

A call from the Chief tells Tracy there is no new information on Deathridge. No word has come from Pat, who went to investigate the funeral parlor. Tracy goes to the morgue and finds Deathridge dead in a chair. One of the coffin lids begins to rise. A hand with a gun appears from within, but it's only Pat, who had been slugged from behind and dumped in a casket. When they return to headquarters they learn that the professor has been bailed out.

Back at his apartment, Starling is packing, obviously in a hurry to get out of town. Splitface raps on his skylight and beckons him to the roof. It's revealed that while Splitface is killing for reasons of his own, Starling is extorting money from the victims before they are

## Morgan Conway delivers a good performance as Dick Tracy.

killed. He offers to split the money with Splitface, but the killer is only interested in keeping Starling quiet. He slashes Starling, who falls through the skylight into his apartment. Tracy arrives on the scene, but Starling dies without talking.

Later, Tracy realizes that the number fourteen refers to twelve jurors and two alternates. He asks the mayor if he was ever a juror. The mayor searches his memory and recalls a case in which a man named Alexis Banning was convicted for murdering his girlfriend. Banning swore revenge on the jury. A check of police files reveals that Banning was scarred in a fight with another prison inmate. A city wide alert is called for his arrest.

Splitface sneaks up on Tracy's house and kidnaps Tess as she talks to Tracy on the phone. Splitface grabs the phone and tells Tracy to call off his cops or he will make off with her.

Junior runs outside and hops onto the rear bumper as Splitface drives off with Tess. Along the way Junior throws off his hat, jacket and shoes as clues. A patrolman spots him and calls Tracy.

Splitface drives to the docks. He takes Tess aboard a boat and Junior follows, but Splitface hears the boy and nabs him. He then ties Tess and Junior up. Tracy and Pat soon follow Junior's trail to the docks and find the boat. Splitface hears them come aboard, but Junior makes a noise to warn Tracy and he breaks through a door and chases Splitface.

Tracy corners Splitface on a stairway and they begin a fight, fall through a railing, land on the ground and continue struggling! Finally Tracy overpowers Splitface and Pat handcuffs the killer.

Tracy and Tess are about to go out to dinner when Pat reports another murder. Once again Dick is off, leaving Tess to wait for his return.

## A good, fast-paced mystery.

Morgan Conway delivers a good performance as Dick Tracy. The film opens with a Crane shot looking down on Splitface as he stands in the shadows. From the beginning, this feature is film noir all the way. Not only are all the sets moody and evocative, but it is set at night. Scenes involving soundstages doubling for exteriors work best for night scenes. They look better shot at night than during the day with special filters.

Anne Jeffreys, who portrays Tess Truehart (brought to the screen here for the first time), delivers a fine performance. She was best known for playing light comedy, as she did for years in the Fifties TV series TOPPER.

Morgan Conway is interesting to watch and brings subtlety to the Tracy role, supported by the tight script by Eric Taylor.

Chester Gould was impressed by Conway's performance and wrote a glowing review for the CHICAGO TRIBUNE at the time. Gould stated, "The gentleman with whom I had shared sweat, blood and tears for almost 15 years, Dick Tracy, is in the flesh, Morgan Conway's flesh, to be exact, right on the screen at the Palace. And for once he did the talking and I listened. I felt pretty helpless, too, because I couldn't use a piece of art gum to change his face or hat, and what he said came from a script and not from a stubby old lead pencil held by yours truly."

We see Dick Tracy's home in this film. It's complete with house-keeper as well as Junior Tracy, thus carrying over several of the comic strip's elements to the screen. Established in this film as an on-going bit, however, is Tracy's inability to keep from letting work interrupt his dates with Tess, even when he's home. That's why she tags along when she can since she'd hardly see him at all otherwise. She's even in Tracy's car when he engages in a high-speed chase after Splitface. The villain had just nearly attacked Tess because Dick had left her alone in the house while he went to search for the fuse box.

This film was later retitled DICK TRACY, DETECTIVE.

# DICK TRACY VS. CUEBALL
## (RKO, 1946)

*In his second and last appearance as Dick Tracy, Morgan Conway turns in a fine performance in a fast-paced mystery with a menacing villain worthy of the newspaper strip.*

Running time: 62 minutes

Executive Producer: Sid Rogel
Screenplay: Dane Lussier and Robert E. Kent
Original Story: Luci Ward
Producer: Herman Schlom
Director: Gordon M. Douglas

## CREDITS
MORGAN CONWAY: DICK TRACY
ANNE JEFFREYS: TESS
LYLE LATELL: PAT
IAN KEITH: VITAMIN FLINTHEART
DICK WESSEL: CUEBALL
ALSO
RITA CORDAY
DOUGLAS WALTON
ESTHER HOWARD
JOSEPH CREHAN
BYRON FOULGER
JIMMY CRANE
MILTON PARSON
SKELTON KNAGGS

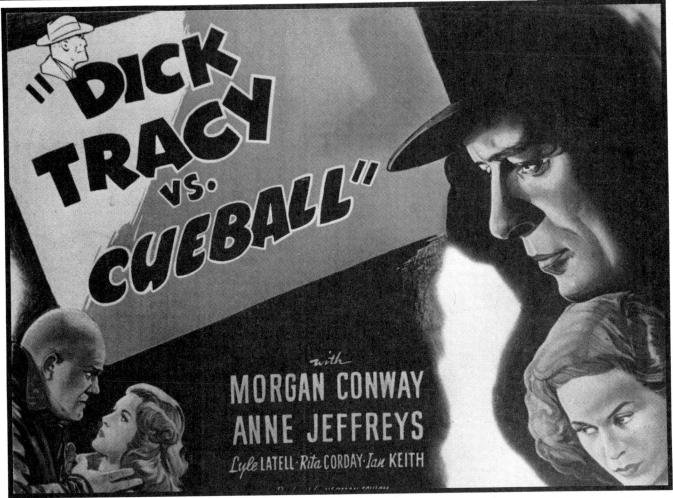

Cueball, a tough looking bald man dressed in black, is standing in the dockside shadows. He puts on a black Western-style hat and joins a group of longshoremen preparing to unload a ship. Instead of following them to the hold, he goes to the passenger quarters, room A12, and startles its occupant, Lester Abbott. Cueball asks for "the diamonds" but Abbott pulls a gun instead. Cueball knocks it out of his hand and strangles him with his leather hatband.

At Dick Tracy's house, Junior discovers that Tess has taken the phone off the hook. Junior replaces the phone and Tracy is called in on the dockside murder. Tess and Vitamin enter with a lit birthday cake for Dick, but he's already gone.

Abbott, the victim, worked for a jeweler named Jules Sparkles. Sparkles' secretary, a Miss Clyde, and a lapidary, Simon Little, are also in Sparkles' office when Tracy and Patton stop by. They have been waiting for Abbott. The diamonds he was bringing into the country were insured for three hundred thousand dollars. Tracy asks for a list of employees who might have known about Abbott's arrival.

Little leaves, followed by Pat. Little goes to another building, where a man named Rudolph informs him, "Mr. Priceless can't make it."

Cueball, however, is there. He wants ten thousand dollars for the diamonds. Little wants out of recutting the stones now that murder is involved. He shows Cueball a secret exit. Cueball threatens the diamond cutter to come up with the money. On the way out, Cueball hits Pat from behind and knocks him out in order to make good his exit unseen.

Meanwhile, Dick Tracy drops Miss Clyde off at her apartment house. As soon as he drives off, she leaves again, but Tracy has parked his car and is following the young woman on foot. She goes to a door, rings and leaves a note. Tracy rings the bell after she leaves and asks the man who answers the door to show him the note.

The man identifies himself as Percival Priceless, a dealer in antiquities. He claims Miss Clyde's note concerns antique candlesticks she has ordered. Tracy pokes around but comes up with nothing, although he sees a newspaper headlining Abbott's murder.

Cueball goes to a bar called The Dripping Dagger. He meets its owner, Filthy Flora. She hasn't seen him since he went to jail ten years earlier. Cueball is looking for a place to hide. She's seen the papers, puts two and two together and demands five hundred dollars rent per night. He hasn't been paid yet but agrees as she maintains a secret hideout in a trap door under the floor.

At the morgue, Tracy finds no clues, but a microscope reveals leather particles in Abbott's neck, right over the "carotid gland."

The next day, Tracy sends Vitamin to the antique shop.

When he arrives, Vitamin claims to be decorating his mausoleum. He says, "I could not enjoy my perennial solitude in the knowledge

MORGAN CONWAY · ANNE JEFFREYS
LYLE LATELL · RITA CORDAY · IAN KEITH

"DICK TRACY vs. CUEBALL"

that there was something imperfect in my surroundings." As Vitamin bluffs his way through, Miss Clyde arrives. Priceless takes her to the back room for her "candlesticks." There she tells him that Tracy is on the case. He tells her that she led Tracy to him.

Cueball wants money, and Little wants out. They need someone else to cut the stones. When Miss Clyde leaves, Vitamin observes that she has no candlesticks, and informs Tracy of this.

That night, Flora delivers a message to Priceless from Cueball. Pat and Tracy follow Priceless to The Dripping Dagger. Tracy covers the front of the dive, Pat the back. Priceless and Cueball meet in the back room. Cueball informs Priceless that he's doubled his price and wants $20,000 before he'll turn over the diamonds.

Tracy enters the bar and strikes up a conversation with Flora. Pat stumbles in the back alley, alerting Cueball. Seeing Tracy in the front, Cueball believes Priceless has brought the police and strangles him. Priceless screams.

Pat breaks in but Cueball kayos him and escapes. A car chase ensues until Pat crashes the police car. Tracy leaves on foot, abandoning his hapless sidekick to contend with an irate beat cop.

Back at the bar, Flora finds Cueball's diamonds stashed under the wash basin. He catches her stealing the gems, kills her and reclaims the diamonds. Tracy finds her body and a scrap of leather beside it.

At Tracy's house, Tess is about to take Junior and his friend, Butch, to the rodeo. Tracy arrives and something about Butch's cowboy costume catches his eye—the braided leather hatband. Junior informs him that these hatbands are popular with the kids, and shows him the magazine ad for them.

Tracy investigates the address and discovers that the hatbands are manufactured by prisoners at a certain penitentiary. A check of recent releases provides identification of Cueball.

Tracy believes Miss Clyde can lead him to Cueball. He has Tess pose as a Miss Belmont to try and buy the diamonds from Clyde. When "Miss Belmont" catches a taxi to this meeting, however, the driver of the cab is Cueball.

Tracy and Patton go to Miss Clyde's place and interrupt an argument between her and Little. Tracy grills them about Miss Belmont. Tess has been taken to Rudolph's place instead of Miss Clyde's. Tracy listens in when Rudolph calls Little and tells him about the girl with Cueball. Tracy and Pat are off.

Cueball tries to get Tess to buy the diamonds, but she says she has no money with her. He grabs her purse and finds a picture of her with Dick Tracy. He advances towards her menacingly with his hatband in his hands.

Tracy races up the stairs, shoots the lock off the door and saves Tess. Cueball escapes, grabs a gun and goes out through the secret exit.

Tracy follows Cueball's cab and shoots out the tires. They wind up at a railroad yard, with Tracy stalking the bald killer through the boxcars. Cueball seems about to escape but catches his foot on a track switch and is crushed under the wheels of an onrushing train.

His case solved, Dick is finally presented with a birthday cake.

Just as vitamin is about to make a long-winded presentation, a patrolman is gunned down right in front of Tracy's house!

Dick Tracy is out the door in a flash. His parting words to Tess are, "Save me some cake!"

## The opening of this film introduces a new continuing motif.

The last scene in the opening credits is a drawing of the villain which dissolves into the actual villain on film.

Another continuing bit introduced in this film is the use of bars with graphic names. In this case it is "The Dripping Dagger."

The actor who played Prof. Starling in DICK TRACY (1945) here plays the jewel courier who is Cueball's first victim.

Character names continue the use of puns from the comic strip, such as the gem dealer named "Jules Sparkle" and the antique dealer named "Percival Priceless."

Vitamin Flintheart is introduced to the films, accurately making the transplant from the comic page. The actor playing him is virtually identical to the likeness in the newspaper strip.

Although Cueball commits one murder after another in this film, none of his victims are innocent citizens. Only his attempt to kill Tess is an attack on an innocent person. This scene stretches things a bit since a civilian would never be used in such a way in a police investigation. A police officer, not the girlfriend of the police detective in charge of the case, would have posed as the jewel buyer!

At one point in the story, a newspaper piece comments on the inability of the police to capture Cueball. In an editorial cartoon on the front page, Dick Tracy is drawn to look like his comic strip incarnation.

Although the script isn't as good as for DICK TRACY (1945), it maintains tension and suspense. It is much better than the last two films in this four-film series. They rely more on gimmicks than craft.

# DICK TRACY'S DILEMMA
## (1947)

Running time: 60 minutes

*In this feature Ralph Byrd returned to the role which made him famous and pursued a vicious foe worthy of the pantheon of Tracy's most vile opponents.*

Screenplay by Robert Stephen Boyd

Produced by Herbert Schlom

Directed by John Rawlins

## CREDITS

RALPH BYRD

LYLE LATELL

KAY CHRISTOPHER

JACK LAMBERT

IAN KEITH

BERNADINE HAYES

JIMMY CONLIN

WILLIAM R. DAVIDSON

TONY BARRETT

RICHARD POWERS

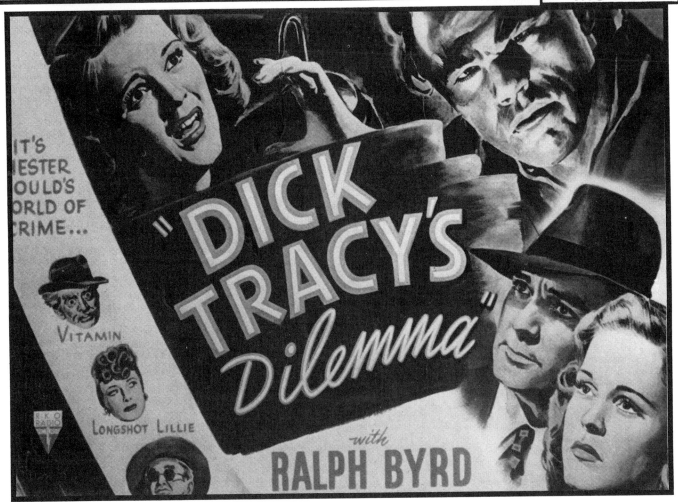

The story opens at night as a brutish, shambling figure in shadows approaches a warehouse. He limps, as if he has a club foot, and keeps his right hand cradled protectively under his jacket. The night watchman, busy preparing coffee over a small stove, is unaware of the intruder's approach. The intruder sneaks up behind him and raises his right arm, revealing a hook instead of a hand. He strikes the hapless watchman over the head. The Claw takes the watchman's keys and then tears the fuses out of the breaker box. His two henchmen then drive up in a truck marked "Daisy Storage." The three go to a walk-in safe and open it. They know the combination. As they suspect, inside lies a fortune in furs.

The night watchman recovers and slowly approaches the safe with his gun drawn. He is about to get the drop on the thieves, but the Claw has circled around the building to keep watch. The Claw hits him from behind a second time, and the robbery proceeds.

Later, a beat cop making his rounds finds the watchman's post abandoned, the lights out and the coffee burning on the stove. He calls headquarters, who calls Car 15, Dick Tracy. Tracy's sidekick Pat takes the call. When he hears the lights are out at the warehouse, he suggests they call an electrician instead of Dick Tracy. The news that the watchman is missing places the case under the homicide department's jurisdiction.

Pat leaves the car and goes into a bar called "The Blinking Skull." Tracy is inside checking the back room for an escaped criminal. After a brief exchange with Jigger, the surly bartender, they leave the saloon.

A pencil-selling beggar named Sightless stakes out the front of the bar. Sightless reveals the falsity of his nickname when he deftly picks a pencil out of the pocket of a passing customer. Tracy stops on his way out, gives Sightless a fiver and asks him to keep an eye on the goings-on in the back room. Sightless protests that he is blind, but Tracy knows of his fraud and uses him as a useful informant.

## This film makes excellent use of moody cinematography

At the scene of the crime, Tracy and Pat review the situation with the patrolman. The warehouse owner, Mr. Humphreys, arrives just as they reach the safe, followed by the vice president of the Honesty Insurance Company, Peter Premium, and his chief investigator, Mr. Cudd. Together they open the safe. The furs are missing and there is blood on the floor. Humphreys expresses surprise that a robbery occurred right after he changed insurance companies. Cudd is uncomfortable with this, but Humphreys insists it's just a coincidence. Tracy receives word that the watchman's body has been found by the road. He heads to the morgue.

The watchman's head had been split by a vicious blow. Among his effects they find a handkerchief with scrawled writing on it. In the lab, they enlarge the writing on a screen for painstaking analysis. From the note, Tracy deduces that there were three thieves in a truck marked "Daisy," and comes up with an incomplete license number. He sends out a bulletin alerting all cars.

Elsewhere the thieves busily switch the plates on the truck and put on a new sign proclaiming, "Rosebud General Delivery." The Claw, a vicious brute, has a fondness for cats that his two partners do not share. They are nervous, since the robbery was coupled with a murder. The Claw insists they must wait until they receive word from their boss. His partners leave their junkyard hide-out and go to the Blinking Skull.

At the Blinking Skull, Sightless is following Tracy's orders. When he approaches the two crooks with his pencils, one of them knocks his cup out of his hand. He follows them inside but cannot find them and is chased out of the bar by Jigger. Sightless goes around to the alley behind the bar, knocks a peephole out of the back wall with one of his pencils and peers in.

The Claw arrives. He and his men argue until the phone rings. The Claw's boss tells him to meet a buyer for the furs at the end of Hemp Street in an hour. Sightless slips, spilling his tray of pencils. The Claw hears the noise and goes to investigate, finding the alley empty except for a few pencils. He chases Sightless down the darkened street and corners him in another alley.

Sightless pounds on the door at the end of the alley but the angry man who opens it will not let him in. He doesn't believe that Sightless is in danger, for the Claw has ducked out of sight. Sightless is about to walk past the Claw, who is waiting with hook raised, when the man opens the door. He says he won't leave until Sightless does. The beggar passes the hidden Claw and catches a taxi to Tracy's house.

At Tracy's house, two people are waiting for him: Tess Truehart and their thespian friend, Vitamin. Vitamin is in the process of mangling Shakespeare when Sightless rings the bell. Vitamin will not let Sightless in, chasing him away without paying attention to his message. When Tracy arrives, he must decipher Vitamin's wordy misinterpretation of the message. This wastes considerable time.

Tracy and Pat stake out Hemp Street but the Claw sees them and leaves. The buyer turns out to be Longshot Lillie, the gambler. Tracy questions her and she claims she was just stopping to light a cigarette. He takes her to police headquarters and questions her some more.

She tells him she doesn't know anything about any furs. When Pat finds twenty thousand dollars under the front seat of her car, she claims to have won it in a poker game. She sticks to this story until Tracy threatens to charge her with the night watchman's murder. Under this pressure, she admits to being involved in the fur buy, but insists she doesn't know who was selling. She simply received an anonymous phone call and decided to take a long shot. Tracy holds her as a material witness.

Meanwhile, Sightless has returned home after his ordeal. He heads for the ice box and chips off some ice to cool his face in front of the fan. When he hears a knock at the door, he drops his icepick. A voice at the door claims to be sent by Dick Tracy. Sightless falls for it.

He finds the Claw waiting at the door with pencils in his hand. Sightless backs into his room and tries to grab the icepick off the floor. He doesn't make it as the Claw claims another life. As Sightless falls, he knocks the fan's plug out of the wall socket. The Claw rises from his deadly work with his face framed in the fan as its blades spin slowly to a stop.

The Claw shambles out into the hallway and starts to call his boss on the pay phone. He dials the number with his hook.

Tracy and Pat enter the building on the floor below. The Claw lets the phone drop and moves quietly up the stairs. The two cops find the body and realize that the killer may still be in the building. They go to call headquarters and find the pay phone off the hook. Tracy calls while Pat heads for the roof.

The Claw catches Pat from behind as he steps through the door to the roof. Pat is stunned but rises to his feet in time to see the killer start down the fire escape ladder. Pat fires several times and wings the Claw before he climbs into his car and escapes. Tracy reaches the roof and berates Pat for firing before reinforcements arrived.

Pat has seen the Claw. He now explains the murder technique and the scratches on the phone dial in the hallway.

At headquarters, Tracy uses an oversized phone dial to learn the first four digits of the phone number the Claw was trying to reach: BA 11. They still need two more digits. Pat's reward for spooking their quarry is the time consuming task of calling every number in town starting with BA 11 until he reaches the Claw's boss.

Pat's description of the criminal has led to a positive identification. They learn that the Claw lost his hand and injured his foot

while a bootlegger when a Coast Guard cutter ran over him.

Pat pitches his voice as low as he can and starts calling, saying, "Hello, this is the Claw." He has a long night ahead of him.

Tracy finds Vitamin in a theatrical depression. He feels responsible for Sightless' murder. Tracy and Tess try to cheer him up but he remains despondent until Tracy comes up with something practical for him to do. Vitamin volunteers enthusiastically.

As Pat continues his thankless task, Tracy goes to see Humphreys. He asks the businessman when the combination on the safe was changed. Humphreys tells him it was changed as a matter of course when the new policy was written. Tracy leaves.

Pat finally gets a result. He calls a number and receives a response but forgets what he dialed. He can't hold the Claw's boss on the line long enough to trace the call.

Tracy goes to the Honesty Insurance Company. Cudd is leaving in a hurry but comes back inside to talk with Tracy and Mr. Premium. Cudd and Premium both admit to knowing the safe combination. The thieves knew the combination, too, but Tracy can't yet deduce who gave it to them.

A sudden noise outside the office alerts Tracy, but it turns out to be Pat, who has figured out what number he called. The man behind the fur robbery is Humphreys, who stands to get a one hundred thousand dollar insurance settlement and his furs back as well.

Pat and Cudd go to Humphreys' apartment while Tracy and Premium wait to see if the thieves will try to sell the furs to the insurance company.

Humphreys tries to reach the Claw at the Blinking Skull, but he's not there. Just as he hangs up the phone, Cudd and Pat arrive. They force their way in and wait for the Claw to call.

Meanwhile, the other two fur thieves find the Claw at the junkyard, wounded and unconscious. They take advantage of his condition to double-cross him, increasing their share of the take. The Claw overhears them. As they leave, one of his cats—a black one—leaps in front of them.

The two men call Premium to make a deal. He is to meet them at the Blinking Skull, alone, with no cops and fifty thousand dollars. Dick Tracy goes in Premium's place.

There's a new blind beggar at the Skull, Vitamin, turning his acting skills (such as they are) to good use. He follows the two double-crossing crooks into the bar and tries to stall the bartender by ordering a lemonade, then sneaks into the back room and hides in a closet. The Claw arrives and surprises his ex-partners. Vitamin listens at the door.

The Claw struggles with one crook. The other one draws a gun and shoots. The fight has shifted and it is the man grappling with the

Claw who is shot and killed. The Claw dispatches the second man with his hook. He then calls Humphreys.

Hemmed in by Pat and Cudd, Humphreys breaks down and tells the Claw of the frame-up.

Vitamin retreats to the closet again as the Claw leaves, but stumbles over a bucket and is discovered. The Claw is about to kill him when Jigger signals. Tracy has arrived.

Tracy finds two bodies, but Vitamin is alive and well. The Claw has escaped. This time, however, Vitamin has remembered what he overheard. Tracy heads for the junkyard.

Tracy tracks the Claw through the shadows of the junkyard. He wings the killer several times and corners him in an electrical substation where warning signs announce, DANGER 33,000 VOLTS! The Claw ducks out of sight behind a transformer as Tracy slowly approaches. He raises his claw to strike. Just as Tracy is about to step into the trap, the Claw brushes against a live wire. The powerful charge casts the shadow of the Claw's writhing death against the wall. The chase is over.

Later, Tracy presents Vitamin with a reward for his brave service in the case of the Claw. The actor is about to launch into a lengthy acceptance speech, but Tracy announces that he and Tess have a dinner engagement.

Just as they are about to leave, news arrives of the sighting of another deadly criminal, and Tracy races off. Tess turns to Vitamin and wishes, with a sigh, that she had been born a super-criminal. When he asks why, she replies, "Because then I might get to see more of Mister Dick Tracy."

## This feature includes a drawing of the villain as the last shot in the opening credits.

The art freezes and fades into the first frame of the film showing the actual Claw. It proves very effective as, in the Dick Tracy tradition, this is a profoundly ugly villain.

This film proves more interesting than DICK TRACY MEETS GRUESOME and makes excellent use of moody cinematography. This was a strong element in DICK TRACY (1945) and DICK TRACY VS. CUEBALL (1946) as well.

This bar is weirdly but not as graphically named. "The Blinking Skull" is a bizarre image nonetheless. It certainly inspires as many thoughts of death as "The Dripping Dagger" and "The Hangman's Knot."

The demise of the Claw is predictable. It was easy to guess his own claw would somehow spell his doom. As soon as they entered the power plant, his ultimate doom became obvious. This is a thrilling mystery although Pat Patton's bumbling incompetence has worn out its welcome.

# DICK TRACY
# MEETS GRUESOME
## (1947)

*Dick Tracy's last big screen outing pitted him against one of the most well-known portrayers of screen villains of all time, Boris Karloff. The match proved less than a classic, but was still offbeat and entertaining.*

## Running time: 65 minutes

Screenplay: Robertson White and Eric Taylor
Story by William H. Graffis and Robert E. Kent
Produced by Herman Schlom
Directed by John Rawlins
Director of Photography: Frank Redman, A.S.C.
Art Directors: Albert S. D'Agostino
Walter E. Keller
Special Effects: Russell A. Cully, A.S.C
Set Decorations: Darrell Silvera
James Altweis
Music: Paul Sawtell
Musical Director: C. Bakaleinikoll

## CREDITS
RALPH BYRD: DICK TRACY
BORIS KARLOFF: GRUESOME
ANNE GWYNNE: TESS
ALSO
EDWARD ASHLEY
JUNE CLAYWORTH
LYLE LATELL
TONY BARRETT
SKELTON KNAGGS
JIM NOLAN
JOSEPH CREHAN
MILTON PARSONS

The story begins with a shot of a hangman's noose in silhouette. The camera pulls back and reveals that it is the sign for a club named The Hangman's Noose. Gruesome approaches the bar cautiously, then goes inside. There people dine and dance to piano music. He asks for Melody.

The piano player, a young man in the Hoagy Carmichael mold (shirtsleeves, hat and lit cigarette all in place), stops playing and greets his old friend. They are former partners in crime and Melody is glad to see him after so long. Melody has been trying to get in on a job but he lacks certain qualifications that Gruesome has to spare. They leave the bar together and Melody promises to introduce Gruesome to the man who has the big job all lined up.

They walk to a building marked "Wood Plastics." A cadaverous man in thick glasses, X-Ray, tells Gruesome to wait in an outer office. Their prospective employer, a mysterious doctor, is working on an experiment. Gruesome sends Melody back to the bar and X-Ray leaves the outer room of the laboratory after warning Gruesome not to touch anything. Gruesome's criminal instincts lead him to case the room. He investigates the contents of an unlocked floor safe. A stoppered test tube catches his attention. When he loosens the cork slightly, a bit of gas escapes. Gruesome drops the vial back into place and staggers to the door, choking.

Gruesome exits the building and returns to the bar, but collapses in the street outside. A beat cop thinks he's stumbled upon a passed out drunk. Upon closer examination, he decides the guy is dead.

## Someone in the film cracks a Boris Karloff joke in reference to Gruesome.

Dick Tracy's sidekick, Pat, happens upon the scene and agrees to take the body downtown in his squad car. When he tries to unload the body, it sits up and gives him a scare. Pat lifts Gruesome's leg back up, which he had previously pressed down, and the stiffened body lies back down again. At police headquarters even Tracy believes the unidentified man is dead.

Tracy and Pat receive a shock when they're called to the morgue and the man on duty announces the body has disappeared. Pat makes an unusual observation, "If I didn't know better, I'd swear we were dealing with Boris Karloff!"

In front of Wood Plastics, Melody and X-Ray are looking for Gruesome. He may have been rendered helpless by the mysterious gas. They are surprised to meet him, fully recovered, coming out of the inner office. The "Doctor" has put him in charge of the entire operation, bumping X-Ray (a disgraced doctor of science) out of the number two spot. X-Ray accepts this stoically.

The gang goes into action the very next day. Just before three o'clock in the afternoon, the three crooks part across the street from the First National Bank. Tess Truehart enters the bank. She tosses paper into a trash can which also contains a gas bomb dropped there by another customer moments before. Tess then walks over to a teller, conducts her business and steps into a phone booth.

Typical bank activities continue around her. One employee chases a cat while the guard pulls the window shade down for closing.

A cloud of white gas begins to escape from the grenade in the waste basket, throwing everyone except Tess into a state of suspended animation. They all freeze into place; even the cat.

Gruesome and Melody enter the bank once the air is clear and proceed to bag all the large denomination money they find. Tess stands in the phone booth pretending to freeze into place. They rush past her, Melody pausing to admire the cut of her figure, then moving on. While the crooks are in the vault, Tess sneaks out of the booth and calls Tracy from another phone in the bank. The one in the first booth wasn't working.

The police are alerted to the crime in progress. As a guard approaches the bank, X-Ray waits in the getaway car and alerts his cronies with the auto horn. They escape, but Melody doesn't like the fact that the guard saw them. He fires, killing the guard, as they drive off.

When Tracy arrives at the bank, everyone inside is still frozen into position. Slowly they return to normal, unaware of what has transpired, much less that there has been a robbery.

When Tracy tells the bank manager of the robbery, he won't believe him until a teller reports one hundred thousand dollars missing from the vault.

At headquarters Tracy ponders the case. If the public learns of the robbery there could be a disastrous run on the banks. Only one reporter is on to the story. Tracy secures his promise to keep it quiet until 2 A.M. This will leave the journalist time to make the morning edition with an exclusive.

Since the police chemist tells Tracy that the mysterious gas defies analysis, Tracy visits the famous physicist, Dr. A. Tomic.

Dr. Tomic is not in his lab, but his assistant, Professor I. M. Learned, is. She tells Tracy that Dr. Tomic has received recent threats on his life and is now missing. Tracy wonders if any of the doctor's formulas are missing as well. Professor Learned agrees to test a formula Tracy picks out from a locked case, but drops the vial on the floor when Tracy mentions the mysterious incident at the bank robbery.

Tracy touches his fingers to the liquid and tastes it, remarking on how much it tastes like water. The professor assures him Dr. Tomic wouldn't store plain water in his safe. Tracy leaves with a sample of the spilled chemical for analysis. He is clearly suspicious.

Once he has left, a worried Prof. Learned makes a frantic phone call.

At The Hangman's Noose, Gruesome takes Melody to task for shooting the guard. X-Ray arrives with payments for the two crooks, but Gruesome isn't satisfied with the money. He tells X-Ray he wants fifty per cent of the take. Before X-Ray can take this ultimatum back to his boss, Tracy and Pat arrive at the saloon. They're looking for Pat's 'walking corpse' as a possible clue to the robbery case.

Gruesome sees the cops and slumps down on the table as if he's passed out to hide his face. Pat still recognizes him. As Pat calls out, X-Ray throws a breaker switch, plunging the bar into darkness and allowing Gruesome and Melody to get out of the bar.

Tracy and Pat pursue them when the two felons pile into a car and drive off. They race through the streets until Tracy shoots out the tires of the getaway car, causing it to crash into a taxidermy shop. Melody is injured but Gruesome escapes into the shop where he eludes Pat, almost skewering the policeman with a spear in the process.

Melody is taken to the police hospital. He lies near death, in a room under constant supervision, his face swathed in bandages.

Tracy assembles everyone who was in the bank at the time of the holdup to try to identify Melody. Some of them think Melody may have been in the bank shortly before the robbery, but only one man is positive.

Tracy fends off the nosy reporter again. He has until 2 A.M. to break the case before the reporter breaks the story.

Professor Learned goes to the park and meets her accomplice, a man named Lee. Lee is the man who identified Melody, but he, not Melody, planted the gas bomb fifteen minutes before the robbery. Learned stole Tomic's formula for Lee, replacing it with the water that Racy tasted in the lab. Lee assures her that the missing Tomic is all right and will return, but she is not reassured. She wants out and is thinking of going to the police.

When she returns home, Tracy is waiting for her, having searched without a warrant. He accuses her of making the water substitution, but she lies and claims Tomic made the switch. Tracy leaves, still suspicious.

Learned is shaken by this encounter and phones Lee again. He agrees to meet her, and to go to the police if it becomes necessary. Gruesome overhears Lee talking on the phone and insists he pick up the woman. When she approaches the car, she detects Tracy trailing her.

She runs to the car and Gruesome guns her down and drives off. Meanwhile, Melody dies in the hospital.

At the plastics lab, Gruesome destroys Tomic's notes—and apparently Dr. Tomic as well— in the incinerator. Lee sets a gas bomb in another room as a trap for Gruesome and tries to lure the killer in with an offer of booze and cigars. Gruesome is suspicious and the plan fails.

X-Ray grabs the bomb and throws it out the window, whereupon Gruesome shoots Lee as he goes for a gun in his desk.

Tracy feeds a fake news item to the radio. Gruesome hears it and believes Melody is alive and about to talk. He decides to kill Melody. He and X-Ray disguise themselves as orderlies and head for the hospital in an old ambulance.

The police are expecting them and allow them to enter the hospital unmolested. Tracy is disguised as Melody by having bandages wrapped around his face. Gruesome and X-Ray set a gas bomb in the room and take "Melody" out on a gurney. Pat is waiting near the hospital to tail the ambulance to the hide-out.

Unfortunately, at the emergency entrance to the hospital, Gruesome gets into an argument with another ambulance driver who recognizes Gruesome and X-Ray as phonies. Gruesome knocks out the driver and decides to steal his newer ambulance. When it exits and drives by, Pat ignores it because it's not the one the felons had arrived in.

## This feature film is shorter than feature length motion pictures we're accustomed to.

At the lab, Gruesome orders X-Ray to stoke the furnace and starts up the conveyer belt to feed combustibles into the incinerator in preparation for the disposal of "Melody." Tracy recovers from the gas bomb just in time, knocks out X-Ray and sheds the bandages. Gruesome hears something and pockets the last two gas grenades. He corners Tracy in a storage room but Tracy escapes through the skylight before Gruesome can toss in one of the bombs.

Making his way to the office, Tracy gets Lee's gun off the floor. The chase is now reversed and Tracy shoots Gruesome, who falls on the conveyer belt feeding the furnace. Tracy stops the belt before the unconscious criminal can be incinerated.

With the case solved, Pat, Tracy and Tess relax in Tracy's office. Tracy and Tess are about to kiss when Pat fumbles with the last gas bomb. It goes off, leaving them frozen inches away from each other just as the reporter is leaving to phone in the story to his paper.

## This time the graphically named bar is called "The Hangman's Knot."

Why would felons who could be facing just such an end want to relax in a place with a name like that?

Someone in the film cracks a Boris Karloff joke in reference to Gruesome, a mixing in of real life more often found in comedies than mysteries. This film has a lighter tone than either DICK TRACY (1945) or DICK TRACY VS. CUEBALL (1946). Even though Boris Karloff is at his menacing best as Gruesome, the script doesn't support him. The film lacks the tension and intensity necessary for his character to be truly frightening. It's a pretty gimmicky story about a gas which puts people briefly into suspended animation.

The screenwriters seemed so taken with their idea they ignored mood and ambiance. It's almost as if they decided to let the returning Ralph Byrd carry the film.

The comic strip style names appear in this film as well, including "Dr. A. Tomic" for a physicist and "Prof. I. M. Learned" for his assistant.

In one scene, when some cornered suspects flee the bar, Tracy shoots at them even though he doesn't know who they are or if they're guilty of anything. That's a bit trigger-happy.

The police artist sketch of "Melody" provided for the witnesses is an incredibly finished drawing considering the subject lies in bed with his head swathed in bandages. Melody's facial bandages were obvious foreshadowing that someone would impersonate him, just as Dick Tracy had another injured suspect in the 1937 serial DICK TRACY.

Much of the entertainment value of this film comes from a Boris Karloff at the height of his powers.

It should be noted this feature, like the other four RKO Dick Tracy features, runs about 65 minutes in length.

# DICK TRACY ON TELEVISION

# DICK TRACY

## (Television-1952)

Television was a new device just starting to make its way into people's homes when Dick Tracy was tapped to make the transfer from the big screen to the small screen. From all reports, the results were mixed.

First aired: September 11, 1950

Last original episode shown: February 12, 1951

### EPISODE ONE

DICK TRACY: Ralph Byrd

SAM CATCHEM: Joe Devlin

HIJACK: Michael Ragan

DOKE: Ward Blackburn

RUFF: Riley Hill

MR. RONES: Bob Rose

Written and Produced by P.K. Palmer

Directed by Willard H. Sheldon

The show begins with a wild shoot-out behind the opening credits. Tracy dispatches all the bad guys. In the first scene, Detective Sam Catchem enters an office and tells the officer on duty about Dick Tracy's latest adventure, the capture of Flattop. Flattop is downstairs in the jail but never appears. The story of his capture, and his plot to kill Dick Tracy for fifty thousand dollars, might have been more interesting if it had actually been shown. Instead it was related verbally by Sam, with occasional interruptions from the stereotyped Irish cop. The conversation finally turns to Tracy's domestic life and both men agree he's lucky to have a wife such as Tess.

Dick Tracy enters. (You can see his shadow outside the set door as if waiting for his cue.) He sits at the desk while the other cops brag over what a great detective he is.

Fade to another scene. Tracy is at the desk sticking pins in a map. He explains to Sam that he is plotting the pattern of a recent rash of car thefts. Eventually the pattern will emerge and he will break the case.

Hijack and Doke drive up to a man with a bag, get out of their car, struggle with him and force him into the vehicle.

After returning to their garage, they take the bag from him. The man, Ruff, wants his money, but Hijack says fifty thousand is too much and will not pay him.

Doke goes out and steals a car and Ruff is forced to work on the car. Doke goes and steals another one. Ruff is unhappy.

It is finally revealed the bag contains tools which can be used to change the serial numbers on the car engines. Hijack has locked the tools in the safe. Ruff swears he'll kill Hijack when he gets the chance.

Doke goes out to steal another car, but it stalls when he starts it. The owner comes out of a building and catches Doke in the act, demanding to know what he's doing. In reply Doke just shoots the man in the arm and drives off.

With his arm in a sling, the man goes to Dick Tracy for help.

Sam remarks, "You're lucky you weren't killed!" Rones replies, "Yes, but I still want my car back."

Tracy asks Rones to show him the area on his map where the robbery took place. Then the three men leave to check the garages in the area, with Rones accompanying Dick and Sam to identify the thief.

Meanwhile, the gang has changed the paint on Rones' car, and Ruff changes the serial numbers. Hijack puts the special tools back in the safe. While he's in the office, Ruff tries to talk Doke into double-crossing Hijack.

Doke likes the idea, but Hijack overhears them. They exchange inconclusive shots just as Tracy and his group arrive.

The newcomers aren't sure if the noise they heard was a gunshot or a car backfiring.

The crooks hear Tracy approach and declare a truce. Hijack and Ruff clear out, leaving Doke to pose as the owner of the garage.

Rones does not recognize Doke or his car. He is certain it isn't his car because of the new color. Doke insists he look at the serial number on the engine. It's different, too, but Rones sees a bit of white paint where he painted his initials on the battery. Doke pulls a gun, enabling Rones to recognize him at last.

Doke is shot dead by Dick Tracy in an exchange of gunfire. Sam observes that he got what he deserved for shooting Rones, and that all crooks who cross Dick Tracy end up one of two ways—in jail or in the morgue. On this cheerful note the story ends.

One can only hope Hijack and Ruff had an opportunity to settle their differences in another episode.

## It is as if no one ever heard of such niceties as editing, pacing or dramatic structure.

### If this episode is any indication, the Dick Tracy television series lacked the production values of the film series. Ralph Byrd walks through the role as if bemused by the almost non-existent plot.

The only excuse for this badly written episode is that the show's producer wrote the teleplay. There was no one to tell him how glaringly awful it was. It's as though the producer only had a passing acquaintance with the comic strip and didn't bother to read it for ideas.

In one sequence Sam and a policeman discuss the capture of Flattop at length. What they recap in conversation is infinitely more interesting than the dull, routine car theft story which follows. The viewer wonders why the capture of Flattop wasn't dramatized instead of the bland police procedural.

It is as if no one involved in the production ever heard of such niceties as editing, pacing or dramatic structure. As Sam and the Irish cop discuss the Flattop case, we're convinced that at any second they'll cut to a flashback of the action. There's no point in having two characters stand there talking. It looks like a locally produced morning talk show.

When Dick Tracy enters, they talk further before the story finally begins. Then, rather than cutting back and forth from the car theft ring to Tracy, the film focuses on three boring crooks until Tracy finally goes out looking for them. Never has television looked worse.

The complete lack of music throughout the episode indicates how cheaply it was made. It was as if they didn't want to go to the expense of acquiring the rights to any of the music used in the previous Dick Tracy films and serials.

The series only lasted twenty-three weeks and supposedly featured other villains with names such as the Mole and the Joker. Unfortunately, after extensive searching, no copies of other episodes could be located.

Ralph Byrd looks just as good as Tracy here as he did in the 1937 serial, but the script gives him nothing to do.

Only the action behind the opening credits is directed with any style. It promises the show will be much more interesting than it is.

Dick Tracy returned in a 1961 Saturday morning cartoon series. In this series Tracy (voice by Everett Sloane) made little more than cameo appearances. The stories actually starred a talking dog, Hemlock Holmes, and a horrible oriental cliche, Joe Jitsu, who made Charlie Chan look conservative in comparison. It ran again in 1971 as part of the ARCHIE'S TV FUNNIES cartoon series.

Tracy also turned up in guest appearances on cartoon specials with Scooby-Doo in the early Seventies. After starring in four serials, four features and a TV series, Tracy couldn't even get top billing when he appeared in cartoon shows! It was an ignominious comedown for the character.

The last attempt to bring Tracy to live-action film before the 1990 motion picture occurred in 1966. William Dozier's Greenway Productions shot an unsold half-hour pilot with Ray MacDonnell as Dick Tracy and Victor Buono as the villain Mr. Memory (created new for the show). Dozier brought both Batman and The Green Hornet to the television screen during the superhero craze of the mid-1960s. Putting cartoon heroes on film was hot.

It took 23 years for the superhero film craze to heat up again. In the wake of Batman and other heroes, Warren Beatty will finally return Dick Tracy to life.

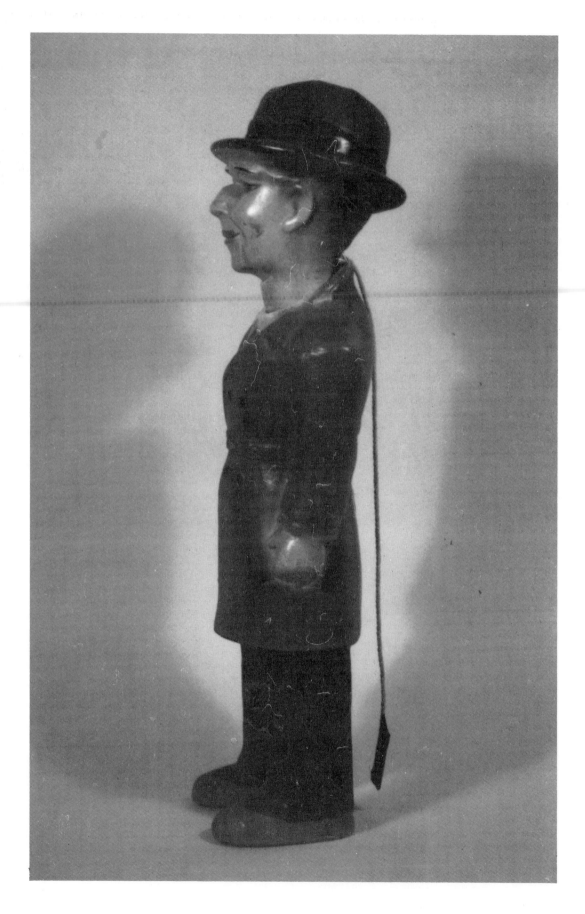

# DICK TRACY COLLECTIBLES

**17.3** Two premium comics given away free as product promotions. At left, a comic from Ray-O-Vac flashlights. The comic at right was an ice cream premium.

*Dick Tracy has been popular with all ages for six decades. Sometimes the strip has been more popular than others, including periods during which it was one of the most licensed properties in the world. Tracy-related products have included every type of book ranging from pop-ups to comics and from novels to comic strip collections. Toys, models, colorforms, cups, banks, paint sets, candy, records, watches and myriad other items have also borne the familiar hawk-nosed visage of the world's most famous comic strip detective. Sparkle Plenty launched her own merchandise bonanza when she was introduced into the comic strip. There is indeed a wide variety of items for the Tracy collector.*

# COLLECTING DICK TRACY

This display of Dick Tracy collectibles would not be possible without the kind assistance of Larry Doucet. Not only did he provide excellent reproducible photographs of some of the rarest items in his collection but he was kind enough to take the time away from writing his own book to pen captions to each of these collectibles. If you enjoy this display you will not want to miss THE AUTHORIZED GUIDE TO DICK TRACY COLLECTIBLES, co-authored by Lawrence Doucet and William Crouch with a foreword by Jean Gould O'Connell, published by Chilton (1 Chilton Way, Radnor, PA 19089). Available in August for $12.95.

All photos from the collection of Larry Doucet.

**7-8  Original art and printed comic cover for HARVEY MONTHLY #128, October 1958.**

**17-13  Covers to Dell Publishing's FOUR COLOR #1, 1939 and the rare FOUR COLOR #8, 1940.**

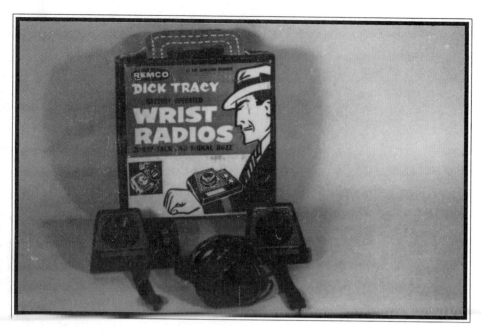

3-32  Remco wrist radio set, circa late 1950s.

**_Dick Tracy and the wrist watch have been intertwined symbols for decades. Perhaps the idea is that when Tracy is on the scene, time is running out for the Rogues Gallery?_**

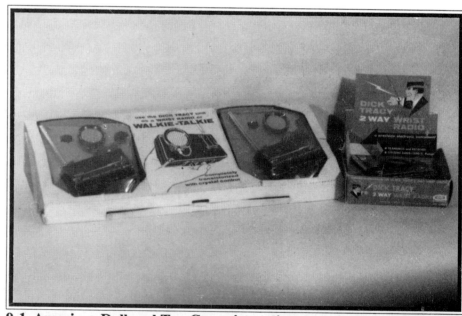

9-1  American Doll and Toy Co. wrist radio set at right. At left, store display for walkie talkie set with power pack and receiver.

**18-34** New Haven wrist watch from the 1930s at left, New Haven animated wrist watch (rocking gun) from 1951 at center and a more modern 1980s wrist watch at right.

**19-18** Bubble packed Laramie spy set from 1969.

13-15 Six of the 144 Caramel Çards (Walter Johnson Candy Co.) from the early 1930s with wrapper shown in center.

19-36 Two Novel Corp. candy boxes from the 1950s. Each box had a different card on the back for collecting. One on left had four-panel strip sequences while the one on the right had a single cartoon panel.

4-24  Five of a set of frosted tumbler glasses issued in the late 1940s. Each tumbler is five inches tall.

# Dick Tracy and food—

# hardly a connection

# that immediately

# comes to mind!

21-5  Kenner Sparkle Paint set from 1963.

**_Things to do with Dick Tracy— you could paint, build a puzzle, make your own comic scene or even paper your walls._**

7-22  Jaymar jigsaw puzzle from 1952— completed size is eleven inches by fourteen inches.

**15-34  Colorforms sets from 1962.**

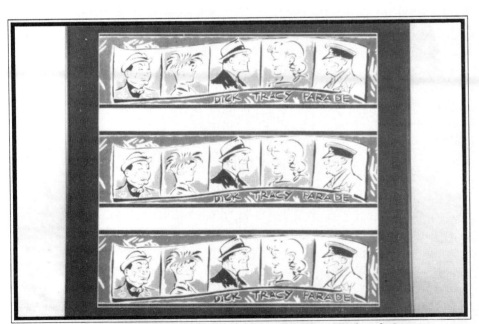

A wallpaper section from the early 1950s. This eighteen inch by eighteen inch pattern of bright colors repeated.

21-13 Aurora model kit of Space Coupe from 1968.

## Three dimensional toys really brought the comic strip to life!

14-15 Marx 11 inch friction car from early 1950s. Lithographed tin car is dark green. Sports a machine gun in the passenger window which emits sparks as well as a battery operated roof light.

5-15 These are the Sparkle Plenty toys, at least some of them! At left is a ceramic bank, a doll from 1947, box back and unpainted ceramic bank are at right with a soap figure and accompanying box in center.

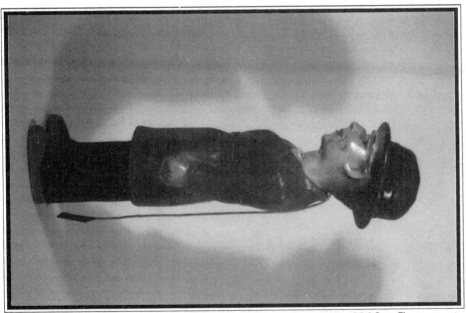

21-26 Thirteen inch composition doll from the early 1930s. Grey coat and green hat. Mouth and head were movable (see the little string?). This is the rarest of all Tracy figurines.

7-33 Tracy was all for voting—but only once to a customer. This US Government Printing Office poster is from 1976. It measures seventeen inches by nine and one-half inches.

*It must have seemed as if everything would eventually sport Tracy's famous face—even greeting cards, posters and records.*

19-24  This Mercury Records double album from 1947 played a radio show broadcast.

**13-3** Norcross greeting and get well cards from the mid 1960s. They sported bright neon colors.

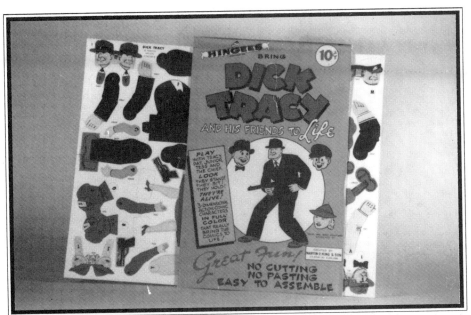

**19-32** Hinges bring Tracy and his friends to life in this 1944 press-out and fold paper set. Each set contains 5 figures of six and one-half inches height. The package measures seven one-half by eleven one-half inches.

15-12  Whitman card game from 1937.

**_Toys and games for those who wanted to get involved in the Tracy action._**

19-5  Marx Sparkling Pop Gum with box circa mid 1930s.

16-19 Marx Target Game from 1941. This ten inch square metal target consisted of a piece of tin with Tracy and friends lithographed on its surface. It came with a rubber-tipped dart pistol. Shoot your hero!

21-8 Ideal Action Playset from 1973 includes twenty colorful carboard figures with stands. The figures measure between three and one-half and five inches in height.

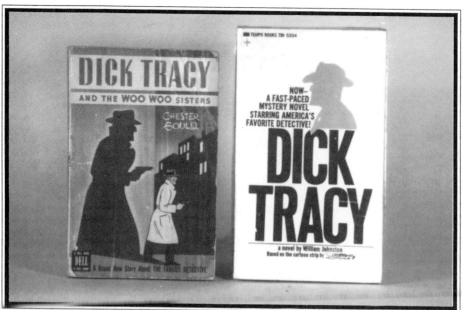

15-17 At left, Dell paparback novel from 1947; at right, the Tempo paperback novel from 1970 with story by William Johnston. Neither book adapted a strip story or offered any illustrations.

17-8 "POP-UP" book from Pleasure Books includes three full color panels that popped out into three dimensional displays when opened. Book measures eight inches by nine one-quarter inches.

# OTHER PIONEER BOOKS

# The World's Only
## Official

# COUCH
# POTATO
# BOOK
# CATALOG ™

**Please note:**
You must be a certified couch potato* to partake of this offering!

\* To become a certified couch potato you must watch a minimum of 25 hours a day at least 8 days per week.

# From Happy Hal...

Star Trek
Gunsmoke
The Man from U.N.C.L.E.

They all evoke golden memories of lost days of decades past. What were you doing when you first saw them?

Were you sitting with your parents and brothers and sisters gathered around a small set in your living room?

Were you in your own apartment just setting out on the wonders of supporting yourself, with all of the many associated fears?

Or were you off at some golden summer camp with all of the associated memories, of course forgetting the plague of mosquitoes and the long, arduous hikes?

The memories of the television show are mixed with the memories of the time in a magical blend that always brings a smile to your face. Hopefully we can help bring some of the smiles to life, lighting up your eyes and heart with our work...

Look inside at the **UNCLE Technical Manual**, the **Star Trek Encyclopedia**, **The Compleat Lost in Space** or the many, many other books about your favorite television shows!

Let me know what you think of our books.

And what you want to see.

It's the only way we can share our love of the wonders of the magic box....

## Selection

**HAL SCHUSTER**

## Administration

**JACK SCHUSTER, COUCH POTATO**

## Customer Service

**PHYLLIS SCHUSTER**

# From The Couch Potato...

I am here working hard on your orders.

Let me tell you about a few new things we have added to help speed up your order. First we are computerizing the way we process your order so that we can more easily look it up if we need to and maintain our customer list. The program will also help us process our shipping information by including weight, location and ordering information which will be essential if you have a question or complaint (Heavens Forbid).

We are now using UPS more than the post office. This helps in many ways including tracing a package if it is lost and in more speedily getting your package to you because they are quicker. . They are also more careful with shipments and they arrive in better condition. UPS costs a little more than post office, This is unfortunate but we feel you will find that it is worth it.

Also please note our new discount program. Discounts range from 5% to 20% off.

So things are looking up in 1988 for Coach Potato.

I really appreciate your orders and time but I really must get back to the tube...

The Phantom
The Green Hornet
The Shadow
The Batman

Each issue of Serials Adventures Presents offers 100 or more pages of pure nostalgic fun for $16.95

SERIALS ADVENTURES MAGAZINE

Flash Gordon Part One
Flash Gordon Part Two
Blackhawk

Each issue of Serials Adventures Presents features a chapter by chapter review of a rare serial combined with biographies of the stars and behind-the-scenes information. Plus rare photos. See the videotapes and read the books!

## UNCLE

### THE U.N.C.L.E. TECHNICAL MANUAL

Every technical device completely detailed and blueprinted, including weapons, communications, weaponry, organization, facitilites... 80 pages. 2 volumes...$9.95 each

## PRISONER

### NUMBER SIX: THE COMPLEAT PRISONER

The most unique and intelligent television series ever aired! Patrick McGoohan's tour-de-force of spies and mental mazes finally explained episode by episode, including an interview with the McGoohan and the complete layout of the real village!...160 pages...$14.95

### THE GREEN HORNET

Daring action adventure with the Green Hornet and Kato. This show appeared before Bruce Lee had achieved popularity but delivered fun, superheroic action. Episode guide and character profiles combine to tell the whole story...120 pages...$14.95

### WILD, WILD, WEST

Is it a Western or a Spy show? We couldn't decide so we're listing it twice. Fantastic adventure, convoluted plots, incredible devices...all set in the wild, wild west! Details of fantastic devices, character profiles and an episode-by-episode guide...120 pages...$17.95

THE COUCH POTATO BOOK CATALOG  5715 N BALSAM, LAS VEGAS, NV  89130

## TREK YEAR 1

The earliest voyages and the creation of the series. An in-depth episode guide, a look at the pilots, interviews, character profiles and more...
160 pages...$10.95

## TREK YEAR 2
## TREK YEAR 3

$12.95 each

## THE ANIMATED TREK

Complete in one volume $14.95

## THE MOVIES

The chronicle of all the movies...
116 pages...$12.95

STAR TREK

## THE LOST YEARS

For the first time anywhere, the exclusive story of the Star Trek series that almost was including a look at every proposed adventure and an interview with the man that would have replaced Spock. Based on interviews and exclusive research...
160 pages...$14.95

## NEXT GENERATION

Complete background of the new series. Complete first season including character profiles and actor biographies...160 pages
...$19.95

## THE TREK ENCYCLOPEDIA

The reference work to Star Trek including complete information on every character, alien race and monster that ever appeared as well as full information on every single person that ever worked on the series from the stars to the stunt doubles from extras to producers, directors, make-up men and cameramen...**over 360 pages. UPDATED EDITION. Now includes planets, ships and devices**...$19.95

## INTERVIEWS ABOARD THE ENTERPRISE

Interviews with the cast and crew  of Star Trek and the Next Generation. From Eddie Murphy to Leonard Nimoy and from Jonathan Frakes to Marina Sirtis. Over 100 pages of your favorites.
$18.95

## THE ULTIMATE TREK

The most spectacular book we have ever offered. This volume completely covers every year of Star Trek, every animated episode and every single movie. Plus biographies, interviews, profiles, and more. Over 560 pages! Hardcover only. Only a few of these left. $75.00

## TREK HANDBOOK and TREK UNIVERSE

The Handbook offers a complete guide to conventions, clubs, fanzines.
The Universe presents a complete guide to every book, comic, record and everything else.
Both volumes are edited by Enterprise Incidents editor James Van Hise. Join a universe of Trek fun!
Handbook...$12.95     Universe...$17.95

## THE CREW BOOK

The crew of the Enterprise including coverage of Kirk, Spock, McCoy, Scotty, Uhura,Chekov, Sulu and all the others...plus starship staffing practices...250 pages...$17.95

## THE MAKING OF THE NEXT GENERATION: SCRIPT TO SCREEN

THIS BOOK WILL NOT BE PRINTED UNTIL APRIL OR MAY. Analysis of every episode in each stage, from initial draft to final filmed script. Includes interviews with the writers and directors. 240 pages...$14.95

THE COUCH POTATO BOOK CATALOG 5715 N BALSAM, LAS VEGAS, NV  89130

THE COUCH POTATO BOOK CATALOG 5715 N BALSAM, LAS VEGAS, NV 89130

## THE FREDDY KRUEGER STORY

The making of the monster. Including interviews with director Wes Craven and star Robert Englund. Plus an interview with Freddy himself! $14.95

## THE ALIENS STORY

Interviews with movie director James Cameron, stars Sigourney Weaver and Michael Biehn and effects people and designers Ron Cobb, Syd Mead, Doug Beswick and lots more!...$14.95

## ROBOCOP

Law enforcement in the future. Includes interviews with the stars, the director, the writer, the special effects people, the storyboard artists and the makeup men! $16.95

## MONSTERLAND'S HORROR IN THE '80s

The definitive book of the horror films of the '80s. Includes interviews with the stars and makers of Aliens, Freddy Krueger, Robocop, Predator, Fright Night, Terminator and all the others! $17.95

## LOST IN SPACE

### THE COMPLEAT LOST IN SPACE
244 PAGES...$17.95

### TRIBUTE BOOK
Interviews with everyone!...$7.95

### TECH MANUAL
Technical diagrams to all of the special ships and devices plus exclusive production artwork....$9.95

## GERRY ANDERSON

### SUPERMARIONATION
Episode guides and character profiles to Capt Scarlet, Stingray, Fireball, Thunderbirds, Supercar and more...240 pages...$17.95

## BEAUTY AND THE BEAST

### THE UNOFFICIAL BEAUTY&BEAST
Complete first season guide including interviews and biographies of the stars. 132 pages $14.95

## DARK SHADOWS

### DARK SHADOWS TRIBUTE BOOK
Interviews, scripts and more... 160 pages...$14.95

### DARK SHADOWS INTERVIEWS BOOK
A special book interviewing the entire cast. $18.95

## DOCTOR WHO THE BAKER YEARS

A complete guide to Tom Baker's seasons as the Doctor including an in-depth episode guide, interviews with the companions and profiles of the characters... 300 pages...$19.95

## THE DOCTOR WHO ENCYCLOPEDIA: THE FOURTH DOCTOR

Encyclopedia of every character, villain and monster of the Baker Years. ..240 pages...$19.95

THE COUCH POTATO BOOK CATALOG 5715 N BALSAM, LAS VEGAS, NV 89130

**Boring, but Necessary Ordering Information!**

**Payment:** All orders must be prepaid by check or money order. Do not send cash. All payments must be made in US funds only.

**Shipping:** We offer several methods of shipment for our product.

Postage is as follows:

For books priced under $10.00— for the first book add $2.50. For each additional book under $10.00 add $1.00. (This is per individual book priced under $10.00, not the order total.)

For books priced over $10.00— for the first book add $3.25. For each additional book over $10.00 add $2.00. (This is per individual book priced over $10.00, not the order total.)

These orders are filled as quickly as possible. Sometimes a book can be delayed if we are temporarily out of stock. You should note on your order whether you prefer us to ship the book as soon as available or send you a merchandise credit good for other TV goodies or send you your money back immediately. Shipments normally take 2 or 3 weeks, but allow up to12 weeks for delivery.

**Special UPS 2 Day Blue Label RUSH SERVICE:** Special service is available for desperate Couch Potatos. These books are shipped within 24 hours of when we receive your order and should take 2 days to get from us to you.

For the first **RUSH SERVICE** book under $10.00 add $4.00. For each additional 1 book under $10.00 and $1.25. (This is per individual book priced under $10.00, not the order total.)

For the first **RUSH SERVICE** book over $10.00 add $6.00. For each additional book over $10.00 add $3.50 per book. (This is per individual book priced over $10.00, not the order total.)

**Canadian and Foreign shipping rates are the same** except that Blue Label RUSH SERVICE is not available. All Canadian and Foreign orders are shipped as books or printed matter.

**DISCOUNTS! DISCOUNTS!** Because your orders are what keep us in business we offer a discount to people that buy a lot of our books as our way of saying thanks. On orders over $25.00 we give a 5% discount. On orders over $50.00 we give a 10% discount. On orders over $100.00 we give a 15% discount. On orders over $150.00 we give a 20% discount. Please list alternates when possible. Please state if you wish a refund or for us to backorder an item if it is not in stock.

**100% satisfaction guaranteed. We value your support.** You will receive a full refund as long as the copy of the book you are not happy with is received back by us in reasonable condition. No questions asked, except we would like to know how we failed you. Refunds and credits are given as soon as we receive back the item you do not want.

Please have mercy on Phyllis and carefully fill out this form in the neatest way you can. Remember, she has to read a lot of them every day and she wants to get it right and keep you happy! You may use a duplicate of this order blank as long as it is clear. **Please don't forget to include payment! And remember, we *love* repeat friends...**

■■■■■■■■■■■■■■■■■■■■■■■■■■**ORDER FORM**■■■■■■■■■■■■■■■■■■■■■■■■■■■■■■■■■■

_____The Phantom $16.95
_____The Green Hornet $16.95
_____The Shadow $16.95
_____Flash Gordon Part One $16.95 _____Part Two $16.95
_____Blackhawk $16.95
_____Batman $16.95
_____The UNCLE Technical Manual One $9.95 _____Two $9.95
_____The Green Hornet Television Book $14.95
_____Number Six The Prisoner Book $14.95
_____The Wild Wild West $17.95
_____Trek Year One $10.95
_____Trek Year Two $12.95
_____Trek Year Three $12.95
_____The Animated Trek $14.95
_____The Movies $12.95
_____Next Generation $19.95
_____The Lost Years $14.95
_____The Trek Encyclopedia $19.95
_____Interviews Aboard The Enterprise $18.95
_____The Ultimate Trek $75.00
_____Trek Handbook $12.95 _____Trek Universe $17.95
_____The Crew Book $17.95
_____The Making of the Next Generation $14.95
_____The Freddy Krueger Story $14.95
_____The Aliens Story $14.95
_____Robocop $16.95
_____Monsterland's Horror in the '80s $17.95
_____The Compleat Lost in Space $17.95
_____Lost in Space Tribute Book $9.95
_____Lost in Space Tech Manual $9.95
_____Supermarionation $17.95
_____The Unofficial Beauty and the Beast $14.95
_____Dark Shadows Tribute Book $14.95
_____Dark Shadows Interview Book $18.95
_____Doctor Who Baker Years $19.95
_____The Doctor Who Encyclopedia:The 4th Doctor $19.95
_____Illustrated Stephen King $12.95
_____Gunsmoke Years $14.95

NAME:_____

STREET:_____

CITY:_____

STATE:_____

ZIP:_____

TOTAL:_____ SHIPPING_____

SEND TO: COUCH POTATO,INC.
5715 N BALSAM, LAS VEGAS, NV 89130

# EXCITING EARLY ISSUES!

If your local comic book specialty store no longer has copies of the early issues you may want to order them directly from us.

**By Roy Crane:**
_Buz Sawyer #1 _Buz Sawyer #2 _Buz Sawyer #3 _Buz Sawyer #4 _Buz Sawyer #5

**By Alex Raymond:**
_Jungle Jim 1_Jungle Jim 2_Jungle Jim 3_Jungle Jim 4 _Jungle Jim 5 _Jungle Jim 6 _Jungle Jim 7
_Rip Kirby #1_Rip Kirby #2_Rip Kirby #3_Rip Kirby #4

**By Lee Falk and Phil Davis:**
_Mandrake #1_Mandrake #2_Mandrake #3_Mandrake #4 _Mandrake #5 _Mandrake #6_Mandrake #7

**By Peter O'Donnell and Jim Holdaway:**
_Modesty1 _Modesty 2_Modesty 3_Modesty 4_Modesty 5 _Modesty#6 _Modesty#7 _Modesty ANNUAL ($5.00)

**By Hal Foster:**
_P V #1_P V #2_P V #3 _P V #4 _P V #5 _P V #6 _P V #7 _P V #8 _P V AN. ($5.00)

**By Archie Goodwin and Al Williamson:**
_Secret Agent #1_Secret Agent #2 _Secret Agent #3 _Secret Agent #4 _Secret Agent #5 _Secret Agent #6

(All about the heroes including interviews with Hal Foster, Lee Falk and Al Williamson:)
___ THE KING COMIC HEROES   $14.95
(The following two book-size collections preserve the original strip format)
___ THE MANDRAKE SUNDAYS   $14.95
___ **THE PHANTOM SUNDAYS    $14.95**

___ (Enclosed) Please enclose $3.00 per comic ordered
and/or $17.95 for THE KING COMIC HEROES
and/or $14.95 for THE MANDRAKE SUNDAYS.
and/or $14.95 for THE PHANTOM SUNDAYS.
Shipping and handling are included.

Name:   _____

Street:   _____

City:   _____

State:   _____

Zip   Code:   _____
**Check or money order only.** No cash please. All payments must be in US funds. Please add $5.00 to foreign orders.
**I  remembered  to  enclose:$_____**
Please send to:
Pioneer, 5715 N. Balsam Rd., Las Vegas, NV 89130